P9-DGV-753

The Axe-Man of
New Orleans

nbm GRAPHIC NOVELS

Nantier • Beall • Minoustchine
NEW YORK

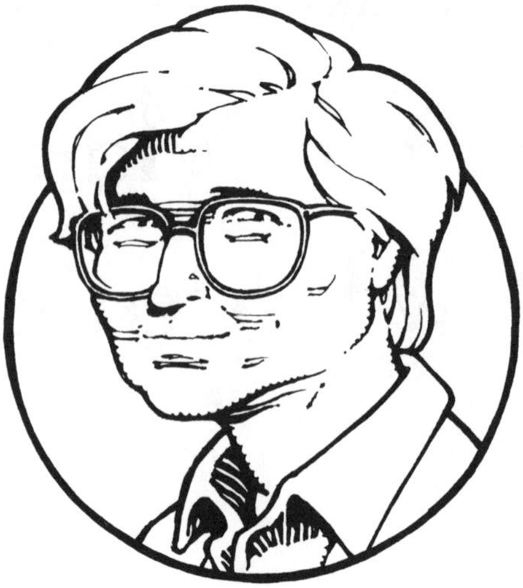

Rick Geary was born in 1946 in Kansas City, Missouri and grew up in Wichita, Kansas. He graduated from the University of Kansas in Lawrence, where his first cartoons were published in the University Daily Kansan.

He worked as staff artist for two weekly papers in Wichita before moving to San Diego in 1975.

He began work in comics in 1977 and was for thirteen years a contributor to the Funny Pages of National Lampoon. His comic stories have also been published in Heavy Metal, Dark Horse Comics and the DC Comics/ Paradox Press Big Books.

During a four-year stay in New York, his illustrations appeared regularly in The New York Times Book Review. His illustration work has also been seen in MAD, Spy, Rolling Stone, The Los Angeles Times, and American Libraries.

He has written and illustrated three children's books based on The Mask for Dark Horse and two Spider-Man children's books for Marvel. His children's comic Society of Horrors ran in Disney Adventures magazine from 1999 to 2006. He's also done comics for Gumby.

In 1989, he started the multi-volume true crime, highly acclaimed series Treasury of Murder with NBM Graphic Novels for which he is mostly known today.

In 2007, after more than thirty years in San Diego, he and his wife Deborah moved to the town of Carrizozo, New Mexico.

Also available wherever e-books are sold

ISBN 978-1-68112-179-6

1st paperback printing December 2018

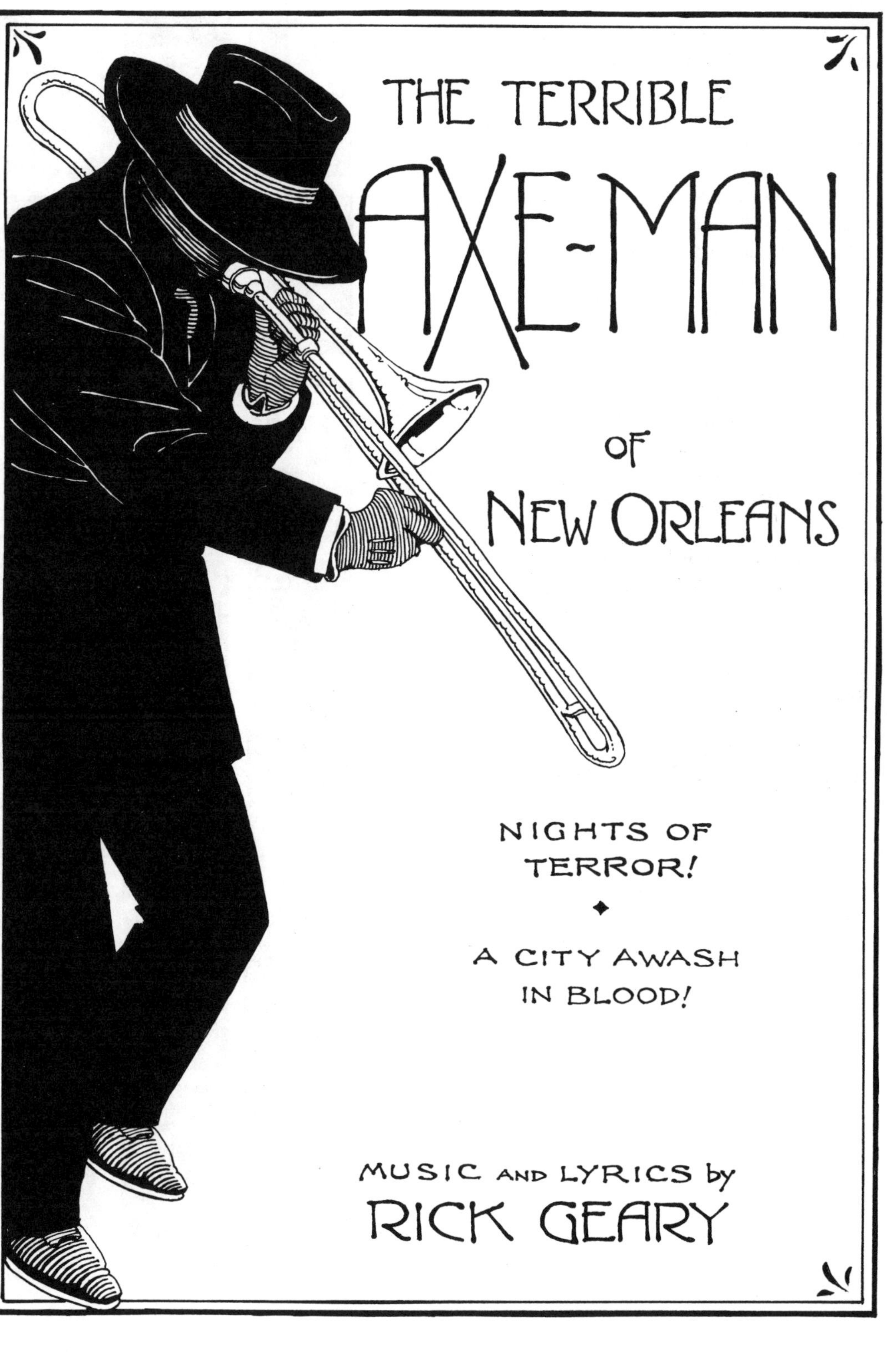

THE TERRIBLE AXE-MAN OF NEW ORLEANS

NIGHTS OF TERROR!

◆

A CITY AWASH IN BLOOD!

MUSIC AND LYRICS by

RICK GEARY

Also available by Geary:
A Treasury of Victorian Murder:
Vol. I, pb., E-book
Jack The Ripper, pb., E-book
The Borden Tragedy, pb.
The Fatal Bullet, pb, E-book
The Mystery of Mary Rogers, pb., E-book
The Beast of Chicago, pb., E-book
The Murder of Abraham Lincoln, pb., hc., E-book
The Bloody Benders, pb., E-book
The Case of Madeleine Smith, pb., hc.
A Treasury of Victorian Murder Compendium I, pb.
A Treasury of Victorian Murder Compendium II, hc.
A Treasury of XXth Century Murder:
The Lindbergh Child, pb.,E-book
Famous Players, pb., hc., E-book
The Axe-Man of New Orleans, hc., pb., E-book
The Lives of Sacco & Vanzetti, pb., E-book
Lovers Lane, hc., E-book
Madison Square Tragedy, hc., E-book
Black Dahlia, pb., E-book
A Treasury of XXth Century Murder Compendium I, hc.
Fiction:
Louise Brooks, Detective, hc., E-book
Biography:
The True Death of Billy the Kid, hc., E-book

see more on these and order at our website:
nbmpub.com

We have over 200 titles
Catalog available upon request
NBM
160 Broadway, Suite 700, East Wing,
New York, NY 10038

A Treasury of Victorian Murder
Jack the Ripper
The Borden Tragedy
Famous Players
Black Dahlia
Louise Brooks Detective
Madison Square Tragedy
True Death Billy the Kid
Rick Geary

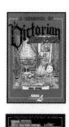

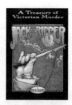

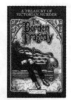

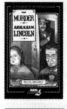

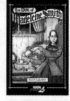

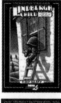

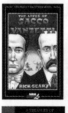

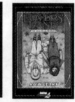

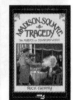

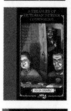

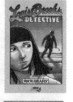

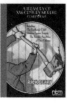

THE TERRIBLE AXE-MAN OF NEW ORLEANS

BIBLIOGRAPHY

Arthur, Stanley Clisby, *Old New Orleans*. (Gretna LA, Pelican Publishing Co., 1995)

New Orleans. (London, Dorling Kindersley Limited, 2005)

Purvis, James, "The Axeman of New Orleans," reprinted in *The Mammoth Book of Murder,* Richard Glyn Jones, ed. (New York, Carroll & Graf Publishers, Inc, 1989)

Saxon, Lyle, Edward Dreyer and Robert Tallant, *Gumbo Ya Ya; Folk Tales of Louisiana*. (Gretna LA, Pelican Publishing Co., 1987)

Schechter, Harold, *The Serial Killer Files*. (New York, Ballantine Books, 2004)

Times-Picayune (New Orleans LA), selected issues, Friday, May 24, 1918-Tuesday, October 28, 1919.

Special thanks to Mark Rosenbohm and Stacey Salamone

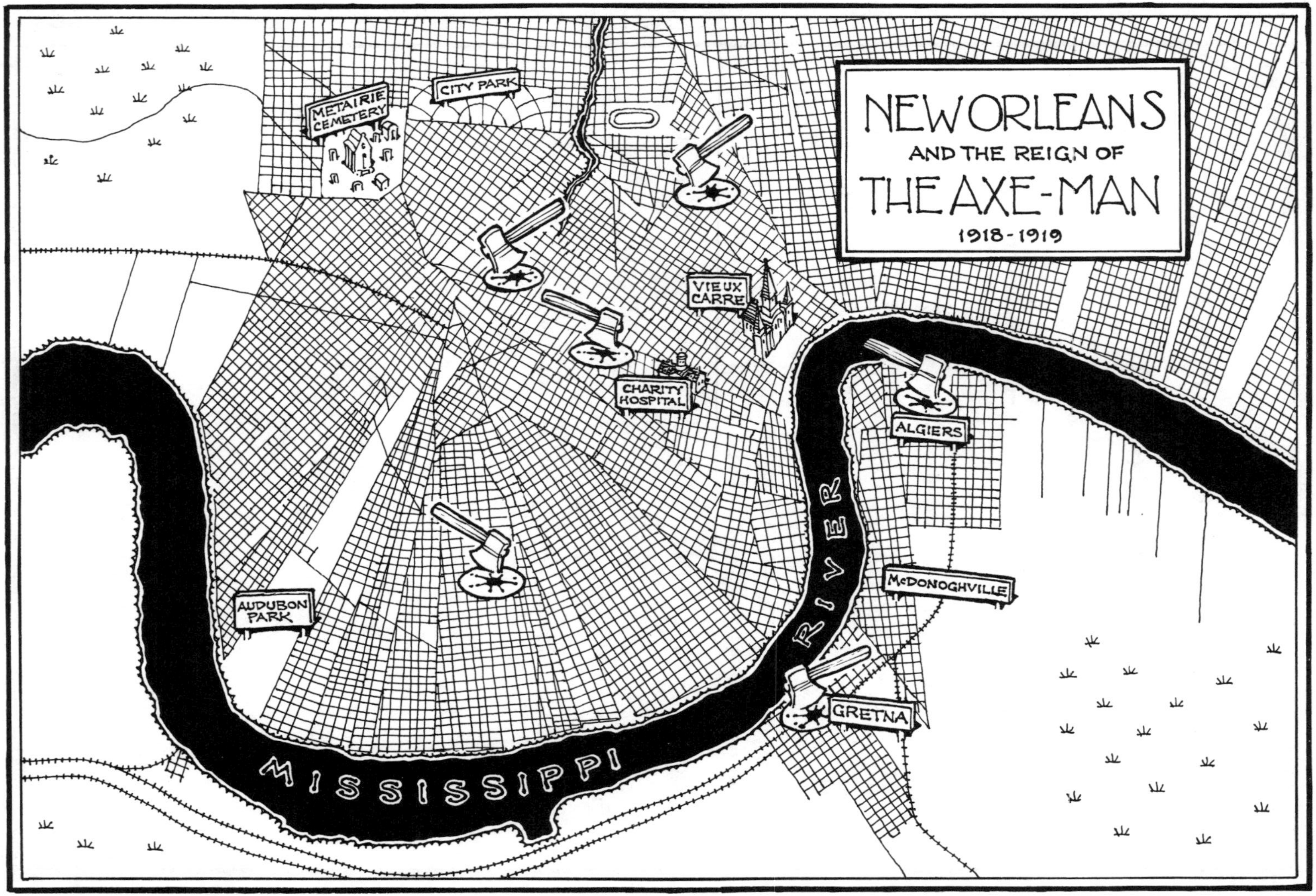
NEW ORLEANS
AND THE REIGN OF
THE AXE-MAN
1918-1919
METAIRIE CEMETERY
CITY PARK
VIEUX CARRE
CHARITY HOSPITAL
AUDUBON PARK
ALGIERS
McDONOGHVILLE
GRETNA
MISSISSIPPI
RIVER

PART I

THE CRESCENT CITY
1918

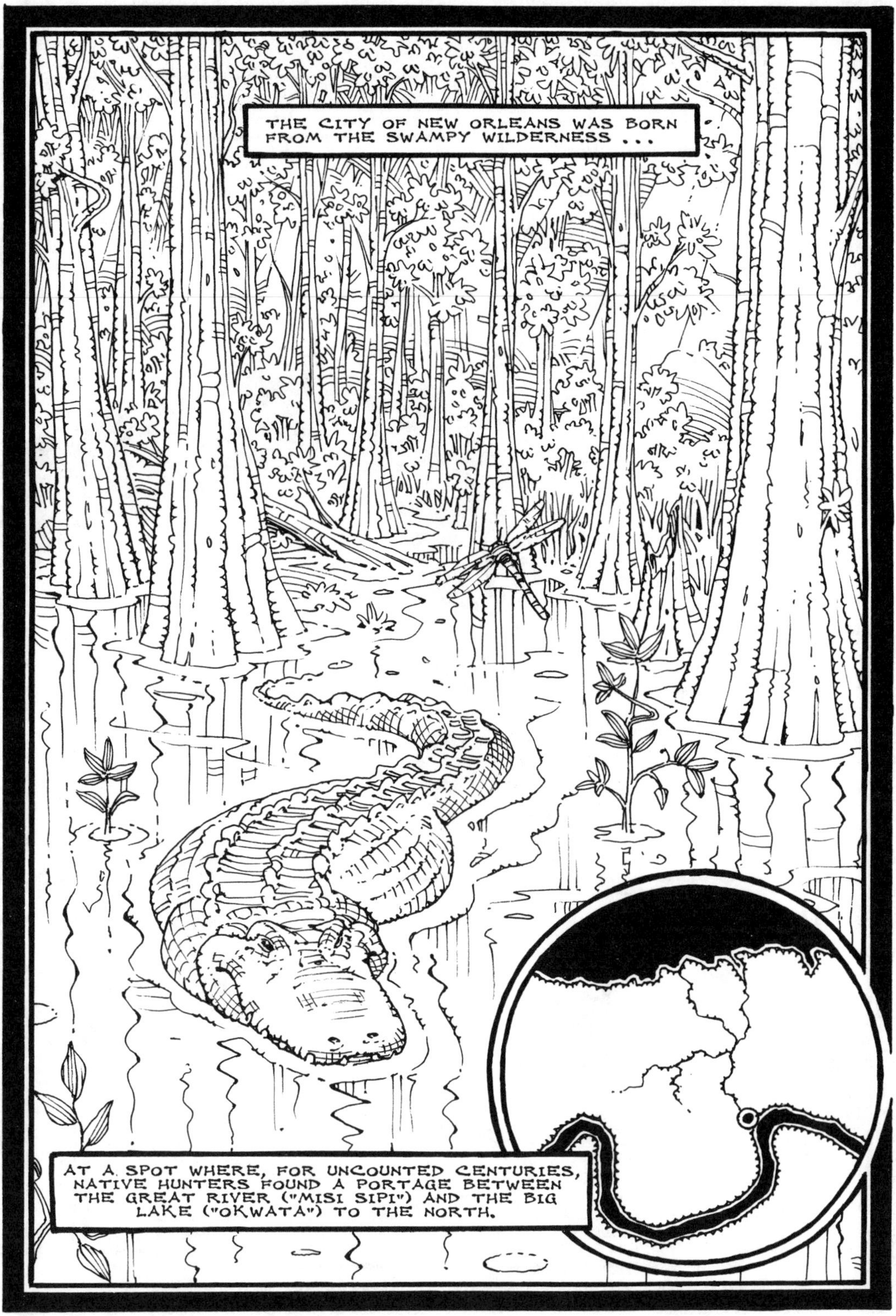
THE CITY OF NEW ORLEANS WAS BORN FROM THE SWAMPY WILDERNESS . . .
AT A SPOT WHERE, FOR UNCOUNTED CENTURIES, NATIVE HUNTERS FOUND A PORTAGE BETWEEN THE GREAT RIVER ("MISI SIPI") AND THE BIG LAKE ("OKWATA") TO THE NORTH.

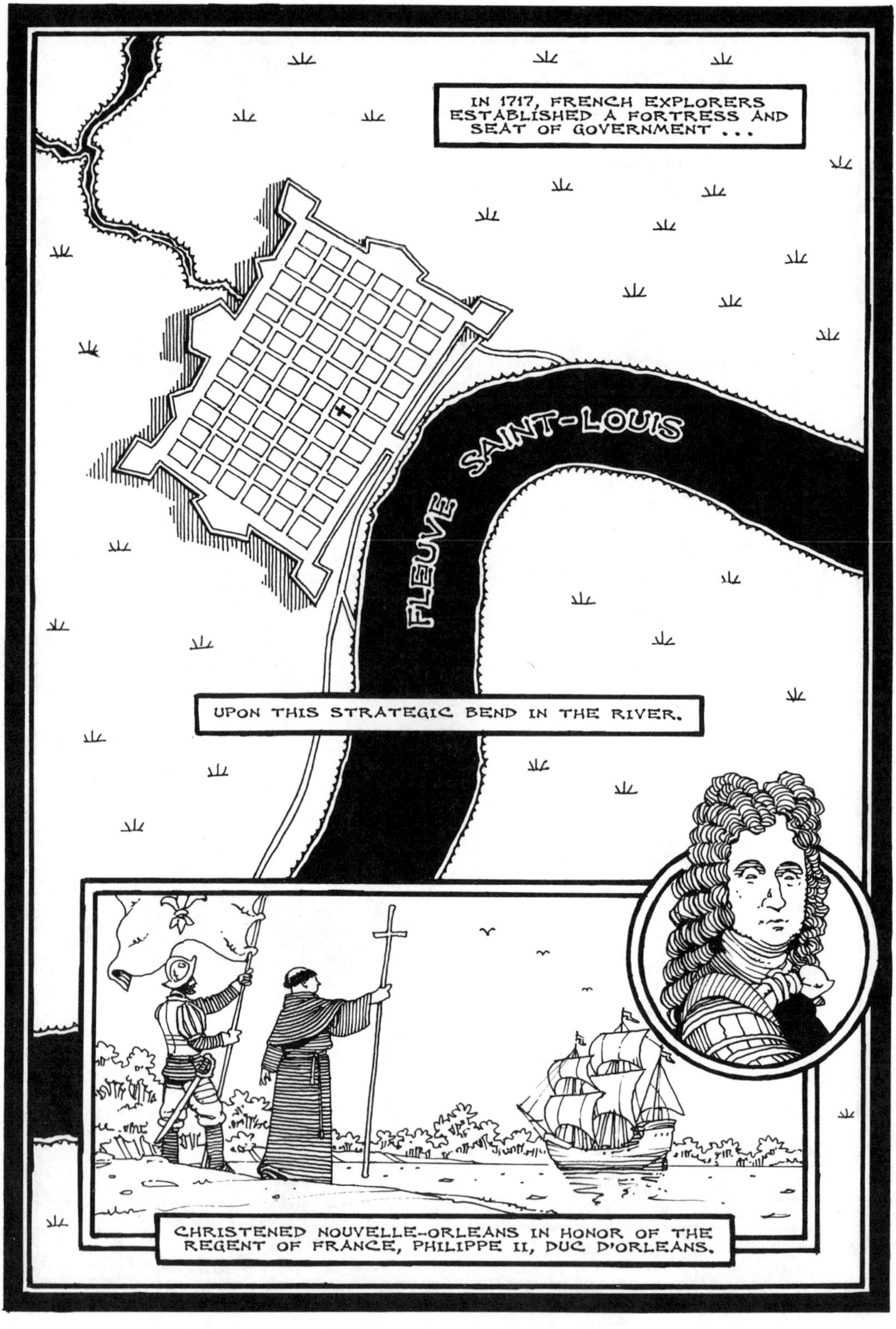

IN 1717, FRENCH EXPLORERS ESTABLISHED A FORTRESS AND SEAT OF GOVERNMENT . . .
FLEUVE SAINT-LOUIS
UPON THIS STRATEGIC BEND IN THE RIVER.
CHRISTENED NOUVELLE-ORLEANS IN HONOR OF THE REGENT OF FRANCE, PHILIPPE II, DUC D'ORLEANS.

IN 1763, FOLLOWING ITS DEFEAT BY THE BRITISH IN THE SEVEN YEARS' WAR, FRANCE WAS COMPELLED TO RELINQUISH MOST OF ITS HOLDINGS IN NORTH AMERICA.

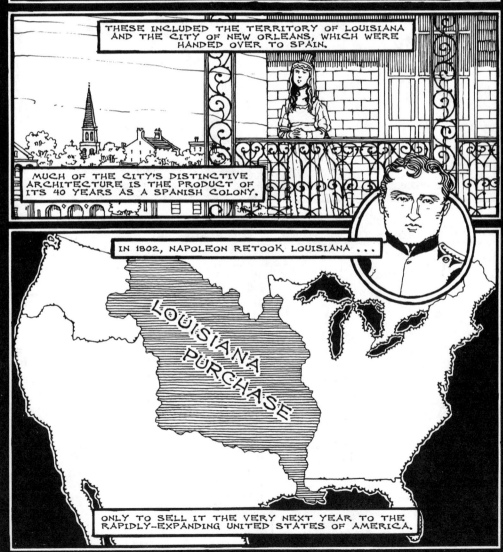

THESE INCLUDED THE TERRITORY OF LOUISIANA AND THE CITY OF NEW ORLEANS, WHICH WERE HANDED OVER TO SPAIN.

MUCH OF THE CITY'S DISTINCTIVE ARCHITECTURE IS THE PRODUCT OF ITS 40 YEARS AS A SPANISH COLONY.

IN 1802, NAPOLEON RETOOK LOUISIANA ...

LOUISIANA PURCHASE

ONLY TO SELL IT THE VERY NEXT YEAR TO THE RAPIDLY-EXPANDING UNITED STATES OF AMERICA.

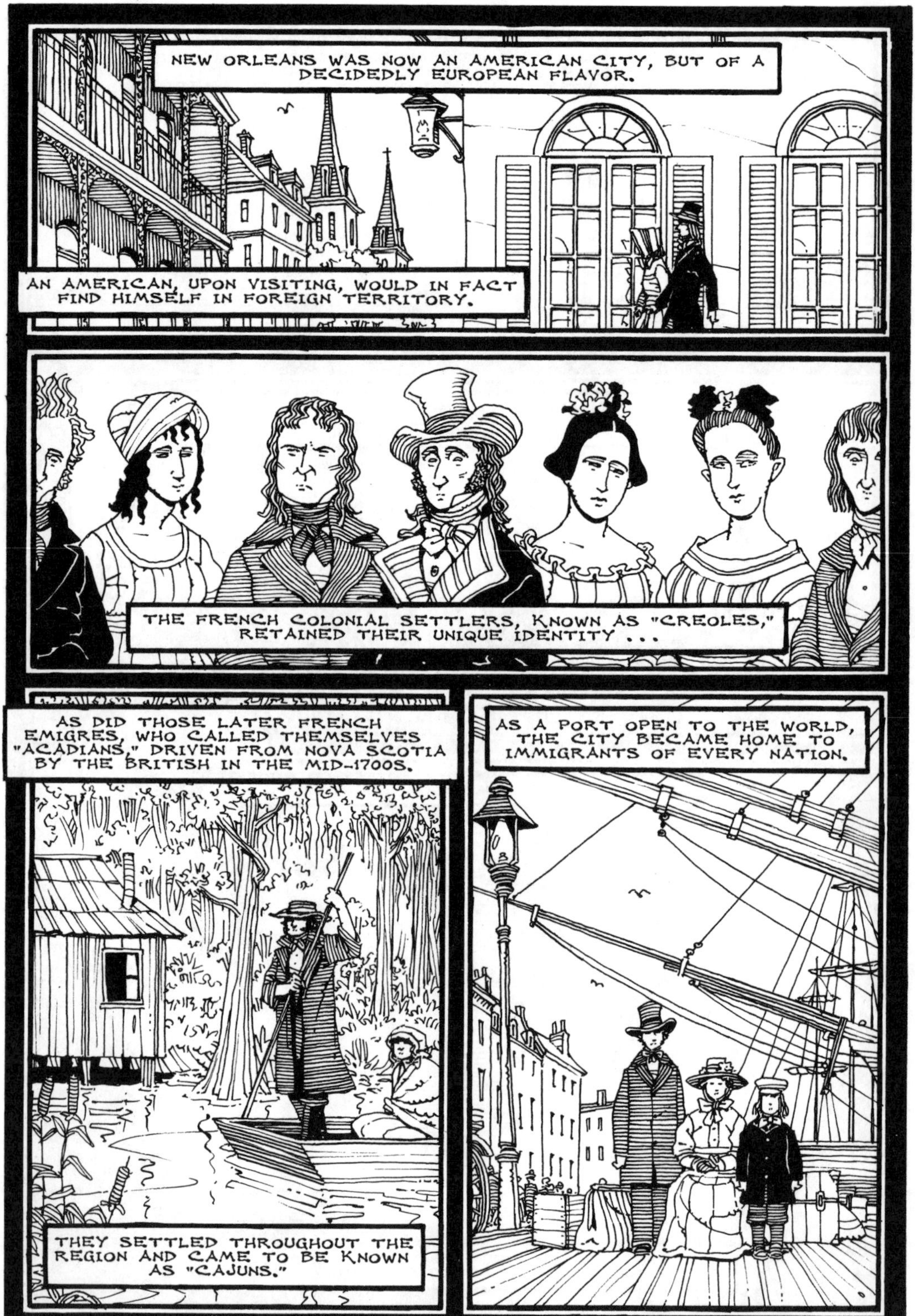
NEW ORLEANS WAS NOW AN AMERICAN CITY, BUT OF A DECIDEDLY EUROPEAN FLAVOR.
AN AMERICAN, UPON VISITING, WOULD IN FACT FIND HIMSELF IN FOREIGN TERRITORY.
THE FRENCH COLONIAL SETTLERS, KNOWN AS "CREOLES," RETAINED THEIR UNIQUE IDENTITY ...
AS DID THOSE LATER FRENCH EMIGRES, WHO CALLED THEMSELVES "ACADIANS," DRIVEN FROM NOVA SCOTIA BY THE BRITISH IN THE MID-1700S.
THEY SETTLED THROUGHOUT THE REGION AND CAME TO BE KNOWN AS "CAJUNS."
AS A PORT OPEN TO THE WORLD, THE CITY BECAME HOME TO IMMIGRANTS OF EVERY NATION.

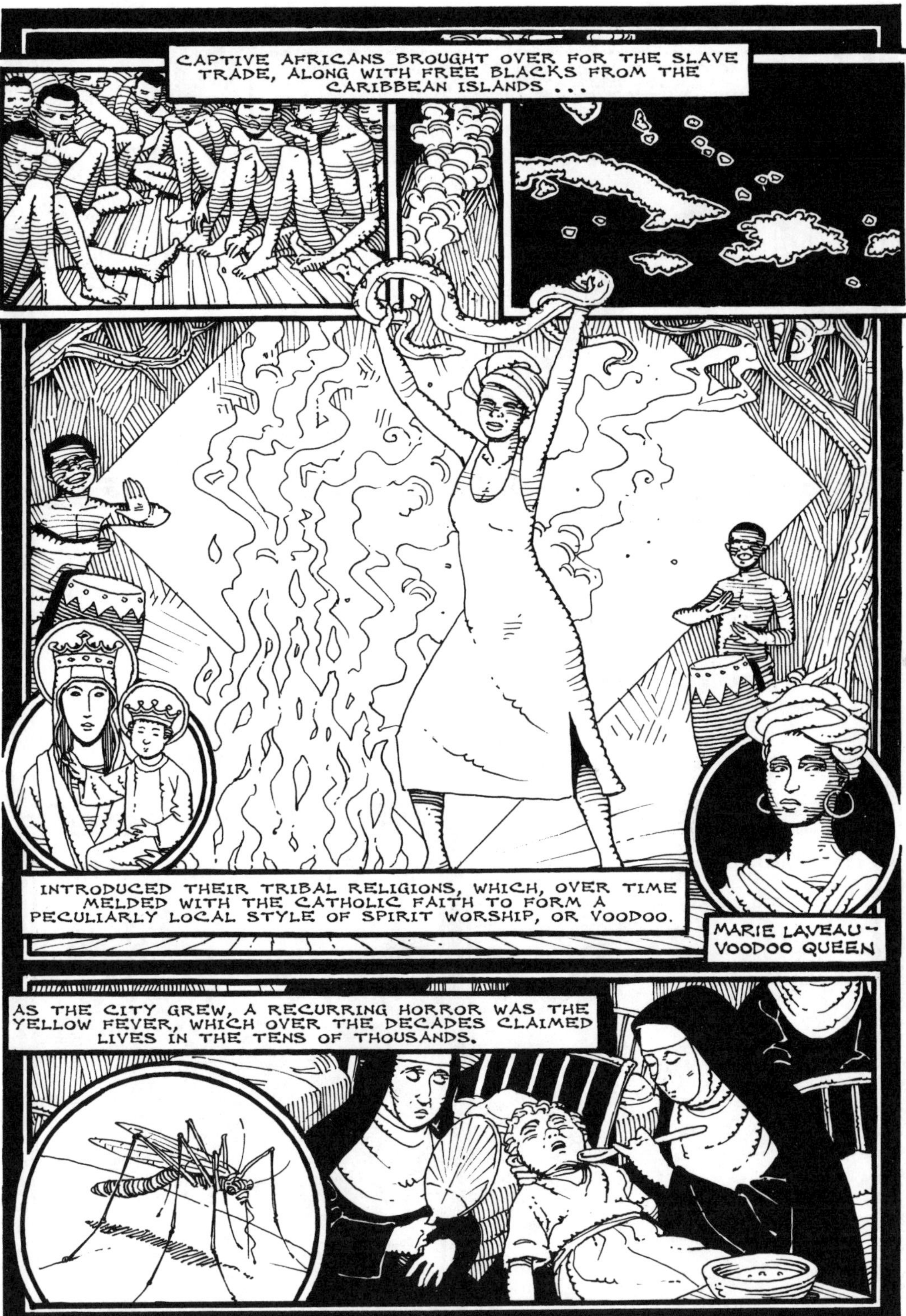
CAPTIVE AFRICANS BROUGHT OVER FOR THE SLAVE TRADE, ALONG WITH FREE BLACKS FROM THE CARIBBEAN ISLANDS . . .
INTRODUCED THEIR TRIBAL RELIGIONS, WHICH, OVER TIME MELDED WITH THE CATHOLIC FAITH TO FORM A PECULIARLY LOCAL STYLE OF SPIRIT WORSHIP, OR VOODOO.
MARIE LAVEAU– VOODOO QUEEN
AS THE CITY GREW, A RECURRING HORROR WAS THE YELLOW FEVER, WHICH OVER THE DECADES CLAIMED LIVES IN THE TENS OF THOUSANDS.

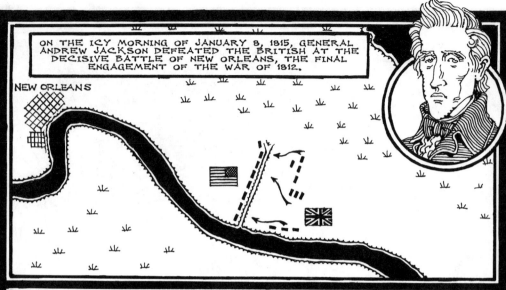

ON THE ICY MORNING OF JANUARY 8, 1815, GENERAL ANDREW JACKSON DEFEATED THE BRITISH AT THE DECISIVE BATTLE OF NEW ORLEANS, THE FINAL ENGAGEMENT OF THE WAR OF 1812.

NEW ORLEANS

THE ENSUING YEARS SAW THE CITY GROW AND PROSPER ASTONISHINGLY

THE COTTON CAPITAL OF THE WORLD!

NATCHEZ

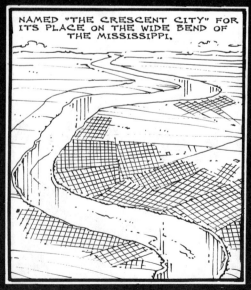

NAMED "THE CRESCENT CITY" FOR ITS PLACE ON THE WIDE BEND OF THE MISSISSIPPI.

BY THE EVE OF THE CIVIL WAR, IT WAS ONE OF THE MOST IMPORTANT STRATEGIC POINTS IN THE ENTIRE NATION.

EARLY ON, HOWEVER, THE UNION SECURED NEW ORLEANS AND OCCUPIED IT FOR THE REMAINDER OF THE CONFLICT.

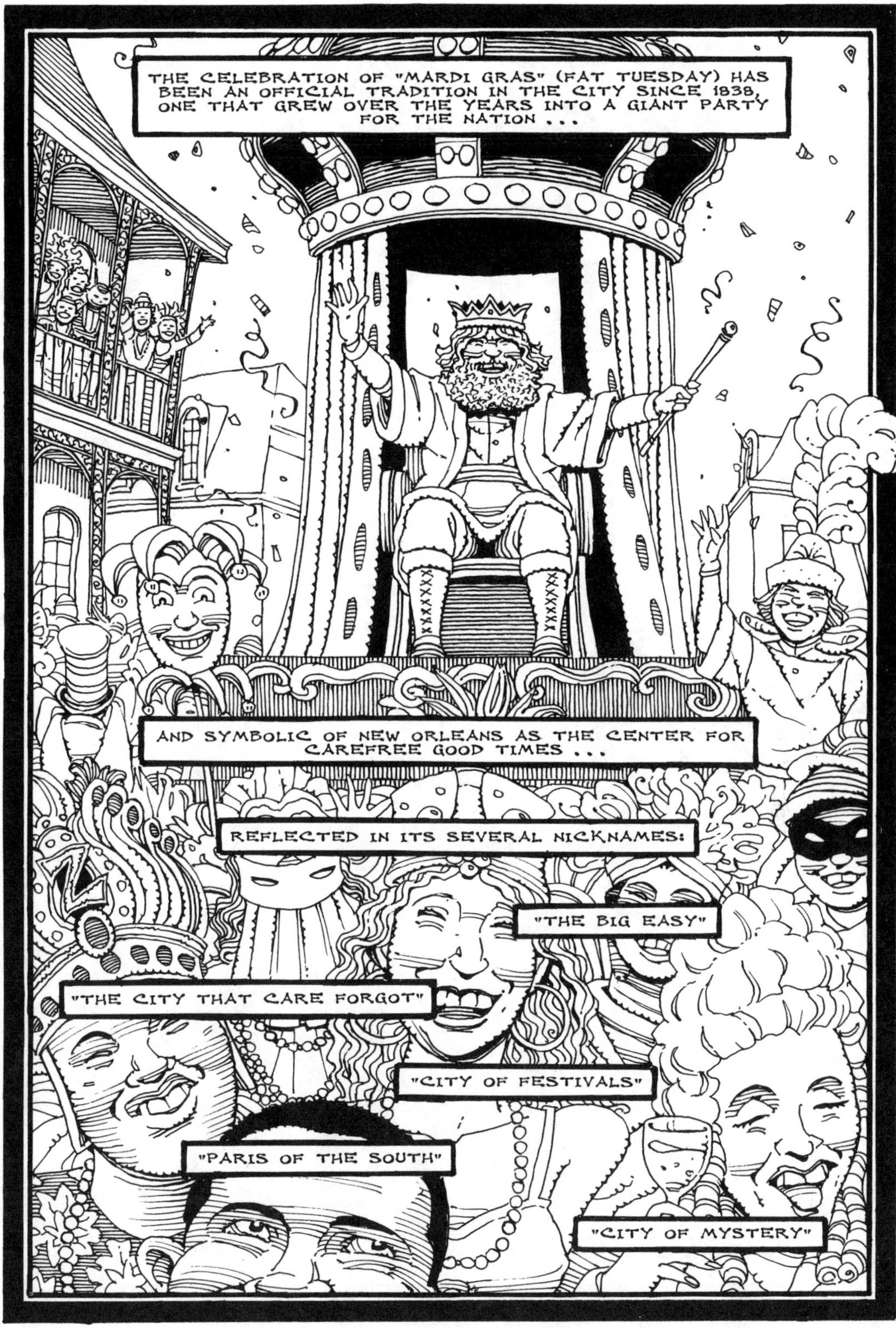
THE CELEBRATION OF "MARDI GRAS" (FAT TUESDAY) HAS BEEN AN OFFICIAL TRADITION IN THE CITY SINCE 1838, ONE THAT GREW OVER THE YEARS INTO A GIANT PARTY FOR THE NATION ...
AND SYMBOLIC OF NEW ORLEANS AS THE CENTER FOR CAREFREE GOOD TIMES ...
REFLECTED IN ITS SEVERAL NICKNAMES:
"THE BIG EASY"
"THE CITY THAT CARE FORGOT"
"CITY OF FESTIVALS"
"PARIS OF THE SOUTH"
"CITY OF MYSTERY"

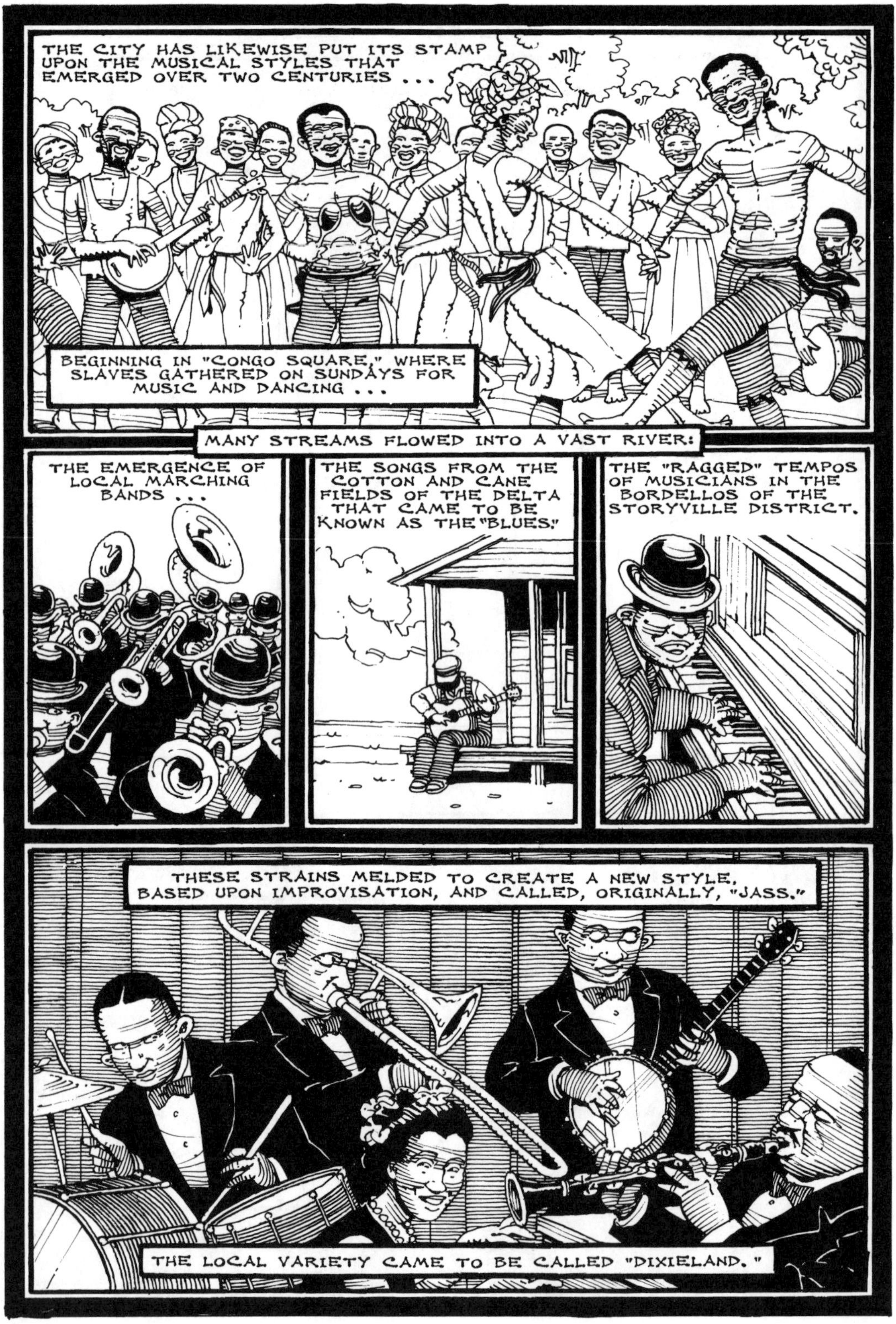
THE CITY HAS LIKEWISE PUT ITS STAMP UPON THE MUSICAL STYLES THAT EMERGED OVER TWO CENTURIES ...
BEGINNING IN "CONGO SQUARE," WHERE SLAVES GATHERED ON SUNDAYS FOR MUSIC AND DANCING ...
MANY STREAMS FLOWED INTO A VAST RIVER:
THE EMERGENCE OF LOCAL MARCHING BANDS ...
THE SONGS FROM THE COTTON AND CANE FIELDS OF THE DELTA THAT CAME TO BE KNOWN AS THE "BLUES."
THE "RAGGED" TEMPOS OF MUSICIANS IN THE BORDELLOS OF THE STORYVILLE DISTRICT.
THESE STRAINS MELDED TO CREATE A NEW STYLE, BASED UPON IMPROVISATION, AND CALLED, ORIGINALLY, "JASS."
THE LOCAL VARIETY CAME TO BE CALLED "DIXIELAND."

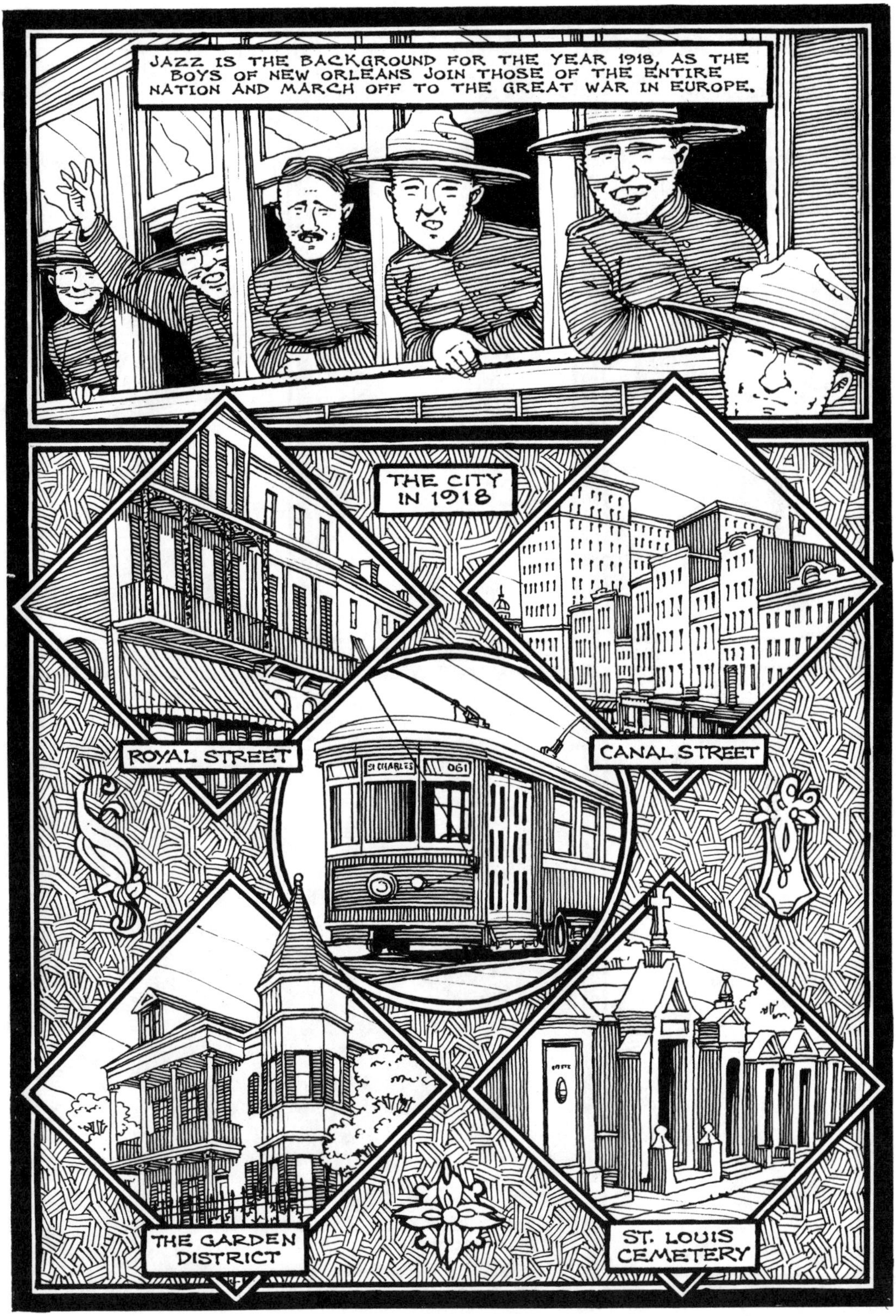
JAZZ IS THE BACKGROUND FOR THE YEAR 1918, AS THE BOYS OF NEW ORLEANS JOIN THOSE OF THE ENTIRE NATION AND MARCH OFF TO THE GREAT WAR IN EUROPE.
THE CITY IN 1918
ROYAL STREET
CANAL STREET
ST CHARLES
061
THE GARDEN DISTRICT
ST. LOUIS CEMETERY

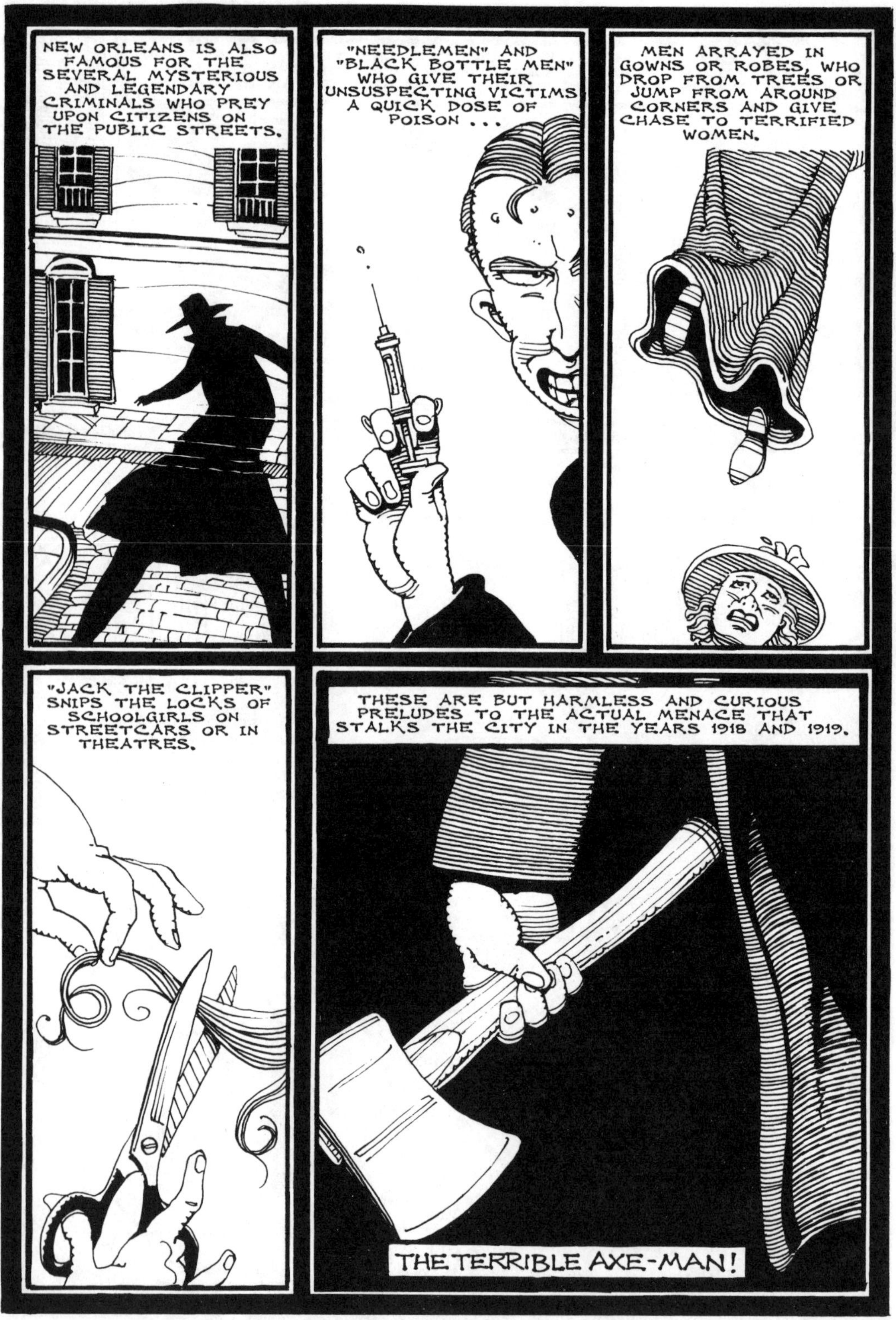
NEW ORLEANS IS ALSO FAMOUS FOR THE SEVERAL MYSTERIOUS AND LEGENDARY CRIMINALS WHO PREY UPON CITIZENS ON THE PUBLIC STREETS.
"NEEDLEMEN" AND "BLACK BOTTLE MEN" WHO GIVE THEIR UNSUSPECTING VICTIMS A QUICK DOSE OF POISON ...
MEN ARRAYED IN GOWNS OR ROBES, WHO DROP FROM TREES OR JUMP FROM AROUND CORNERS AND GIVE CHASE TO TERRIFIED WOMEN.
"JACK THE CLIPPER" SNIPS THE LOCKS OF SCHOOLGIRLS ON STREETCARS OR IN THEATRES.
THESE ARE BUT HARMLESS AND CURIOUS PRELUDES TO THE ACTUAL MENACE THAT STALKS THE CITY IN THE YEARS 1918 AND 1919.
THE TERRIBLE AXE-MAN!

PART II

BLOOD EVERYWHERE!

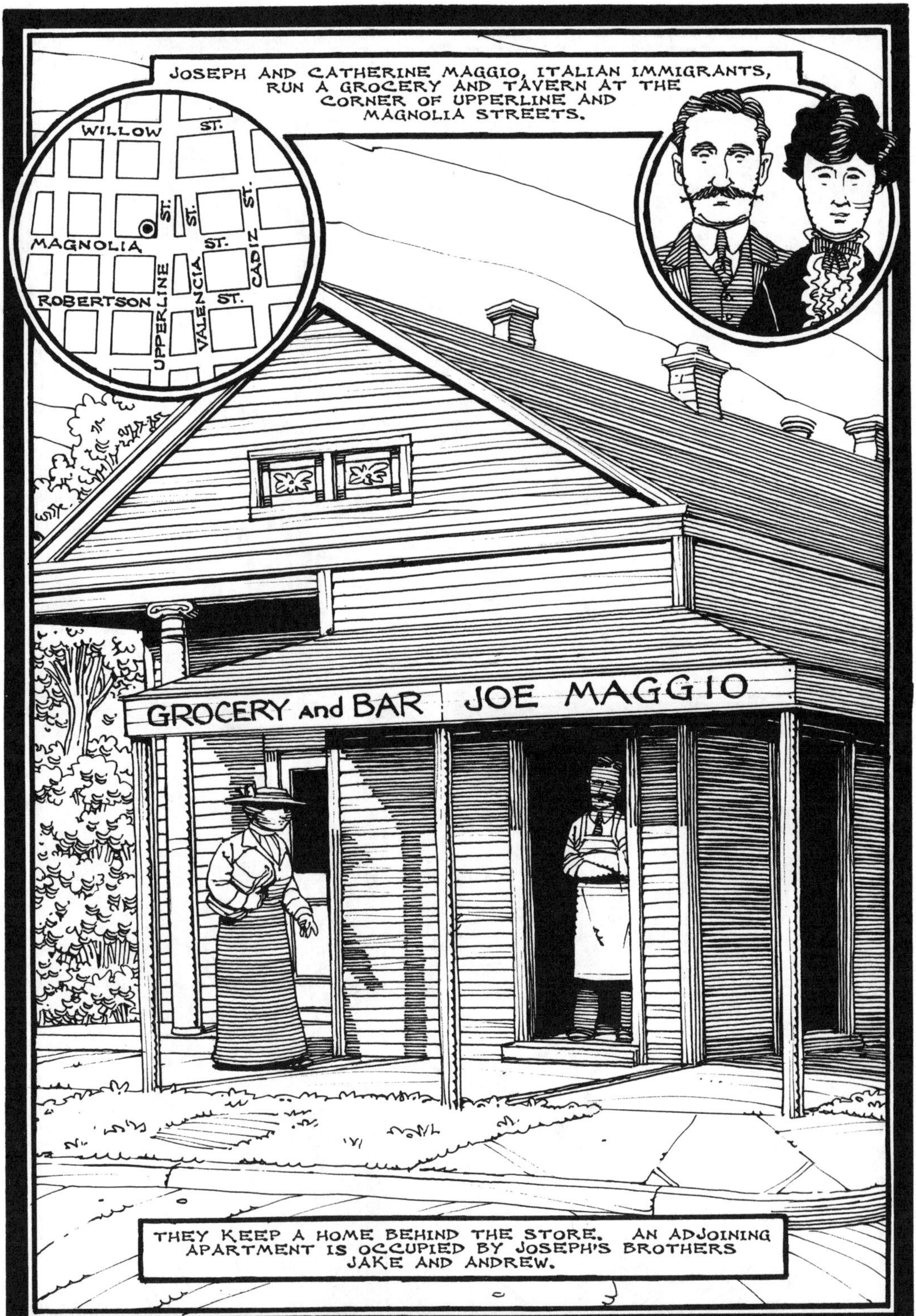
JOSEPH AND CATHERINE MAGGIO, ITALIAN IMMIGRANTS, RUN A GROCERY AND TAVERN AT THE CORNER OF UPPERLINE AND MAGNOLIA STREETS.
WILLOW ST.
MAGNOLIA ST.
ROBERTSON ST.
UPPERLINE ST.
VALENCIA ST.
CADIZ ST.
GROCERY and BAR
JOE MAGGIO
THEY KEEP A HOME BEHIND THE STORE. AN ADJOINING APARTMENT IS OCCUPIED BY JOSEPH'S BROTHERS JAKE AND ANDREW.

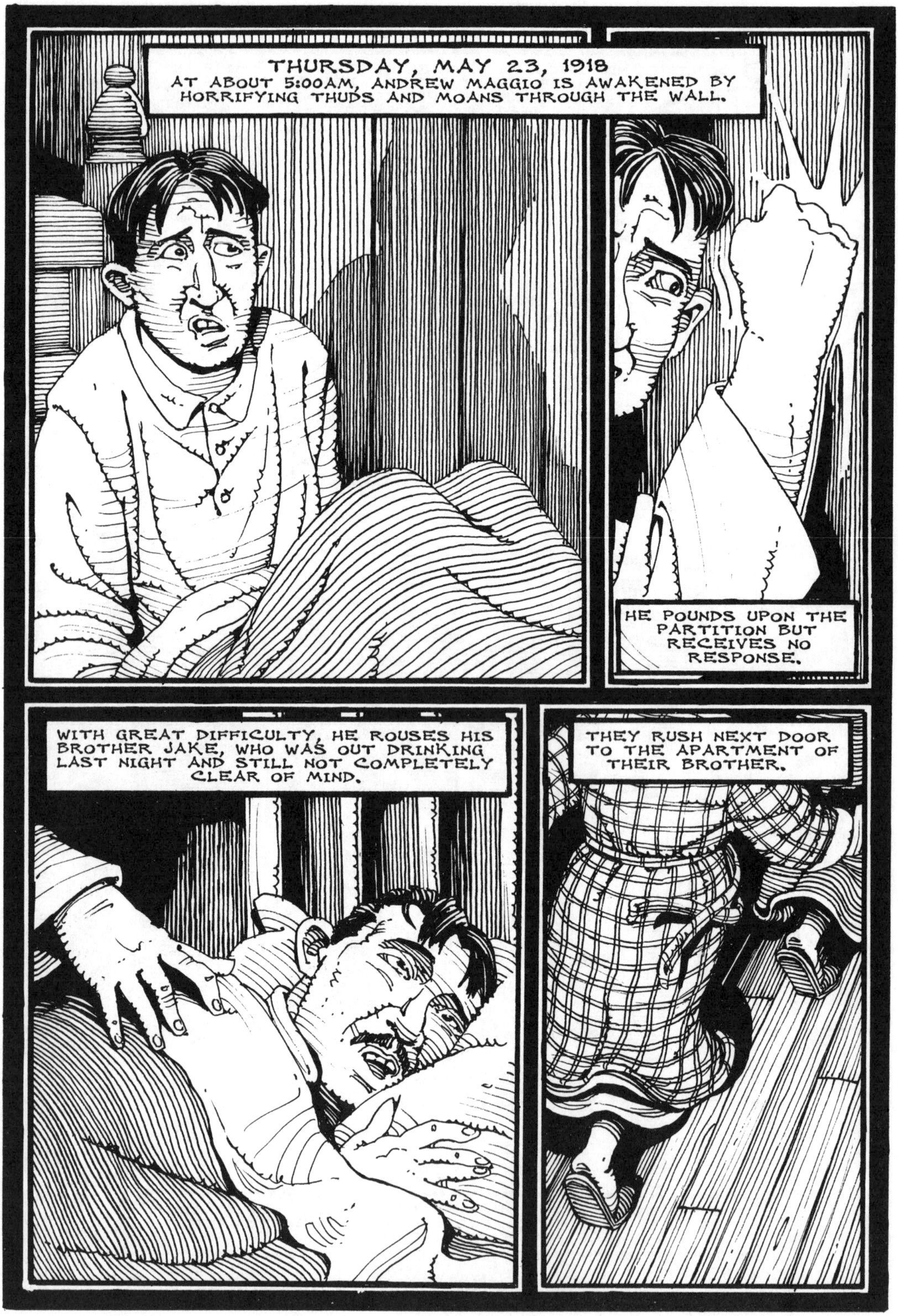
THURSDAY, MAY 23, 1918
AT ABOUT 5:00AM, ANDREW MAGGIO IS AWAKENED BY HORRIFYING THUDS AND MOANS THROUGH THE WALL.
HE POUNDS UPON THE PARTITION BUT RECEIVES NO RESPONSE.
WITH GREAT DIFFICULTY, HE ROUSES HIS BROTHER JAKE, WHO WAS OUT DRINKING LAST NIGHT AND STILL NOT COMPLETELY CLEAR OF MIND.
THEY RUSH NEXT DOOR TO THE APARTMENT OF THEIR BROTHER.

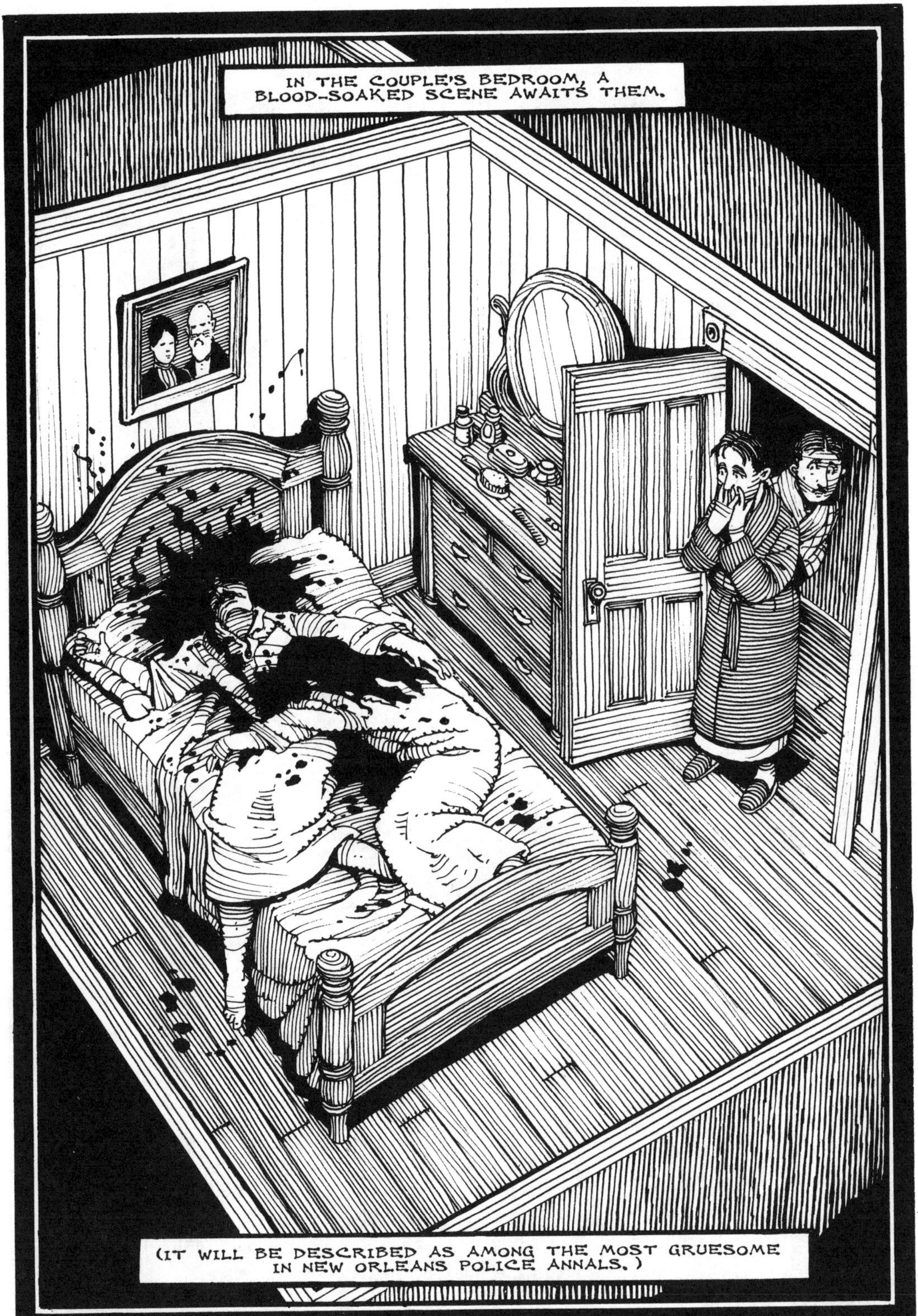
IN THE COUPLE'S BEDROOM, A BLOOD-SOAKED SCENE AWAITS THEM.
(IT WILL BE DESCRIBED AS AMONG THE MOST GRUESOME IN NEW ORLEANS POLICE ANNALS.)

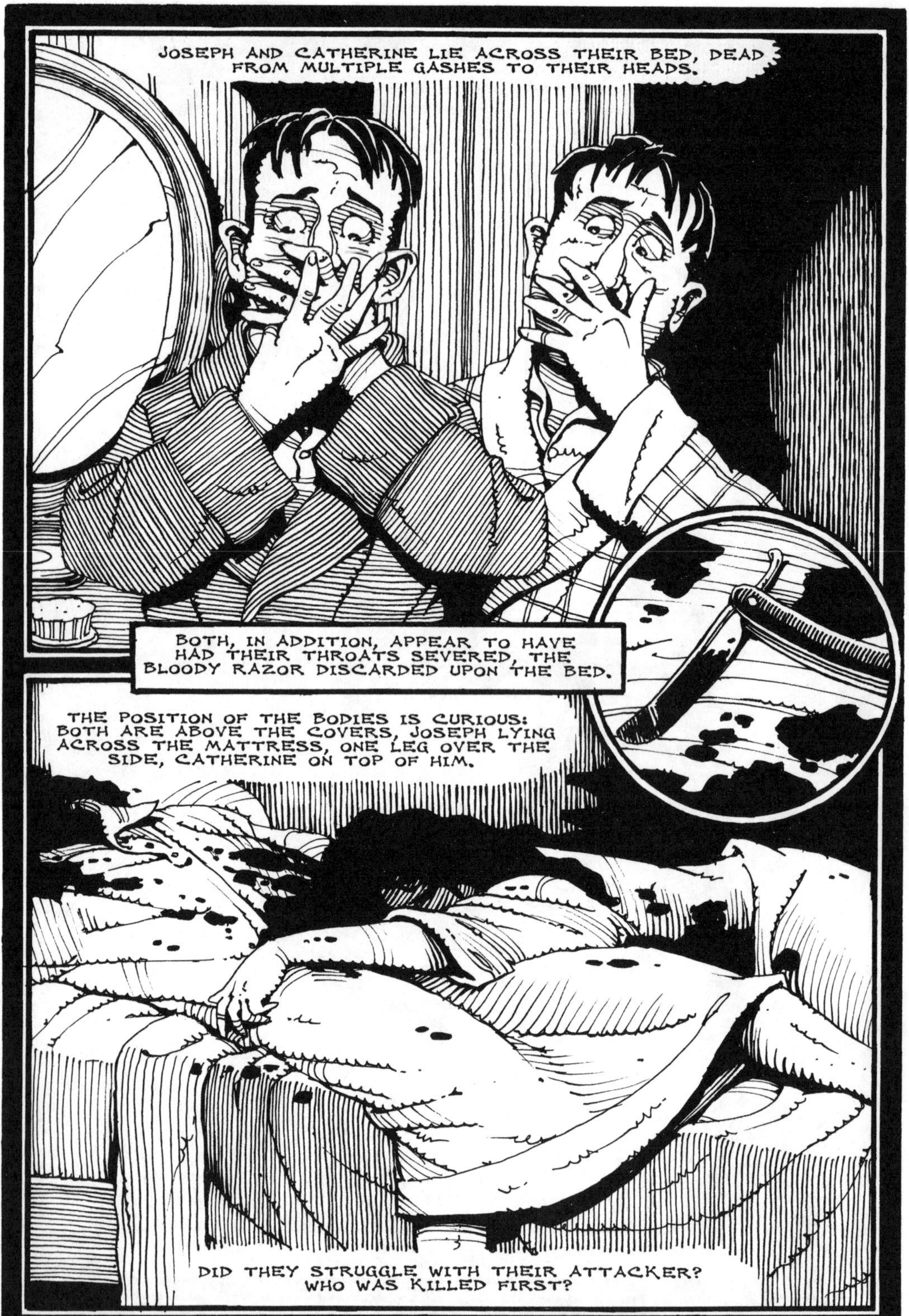
JOSEPH AND CATHERINE LIE ACROSS THEIR BED, DEAD FROM MULTIPLE GASHES TO THEIR HEADS.
BOTH, IN ADDITION, APPEAR TO HAVE HAD THEIR THROATS SEVERED, THE BLOODY RAZOR DISCARDED UPON THE BED.
THE POSITION OF THE BODIES IS CURIOUS: BOTH ARE ABOVE THE COVERS, JOSEPH LYING ACROSS THE MATTRESS, ONE LEG OVER THE SIDE, CATHERINE ON TOP OF HIM.
DID THEY STRUGGLE WITH THEIR ATTACKER? WHO WAS KILLED FIRST?

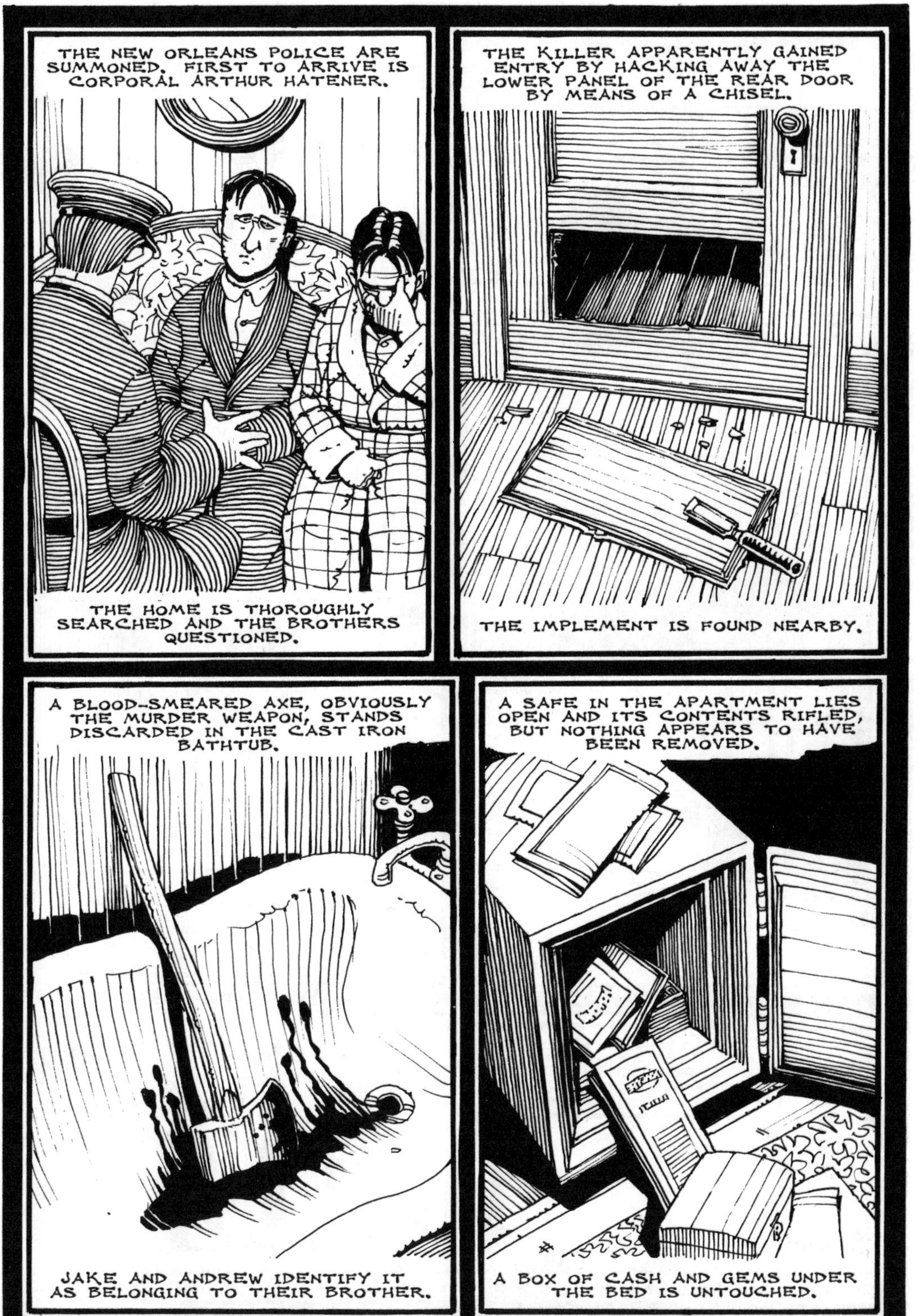
THE NEW ORLEANS POLICE ARE SUMMONED. FIRST TO ARRIVE IS CORPORAL ARTHUR HATENER.
THE HOME IS THOROUGHLY SEARCHED AND THE BROTHERS QUESTIONED.
THE KILLER APPARENTLY GAINED ENTRY BY HACKING AWAY THE LOWER PANEL OF THE REAR DOOR BY MEANS OF A CHISEL.
THE IMPLEMENT IS FOUND NEARBY.
A BLOOD-SMEARED AXE, OBVIOUSLY THE MURDER WEAPON, STANDS DISCARDED IN THE CAST IRON BATHTUB.
JAKE AND ANDREW IDENTIFY IT AS BELONGING TO THEIR BROTHER.
A SAFE IN THE APARTMENT LIES OPEN AND ITS CONTENTS RIFLED, BUT NOTHING APPEARS TO HAVE BEEN REMOVED.
A BOX OF CASH AND GEMS UNDER THE BED IS UNTOUCHED.

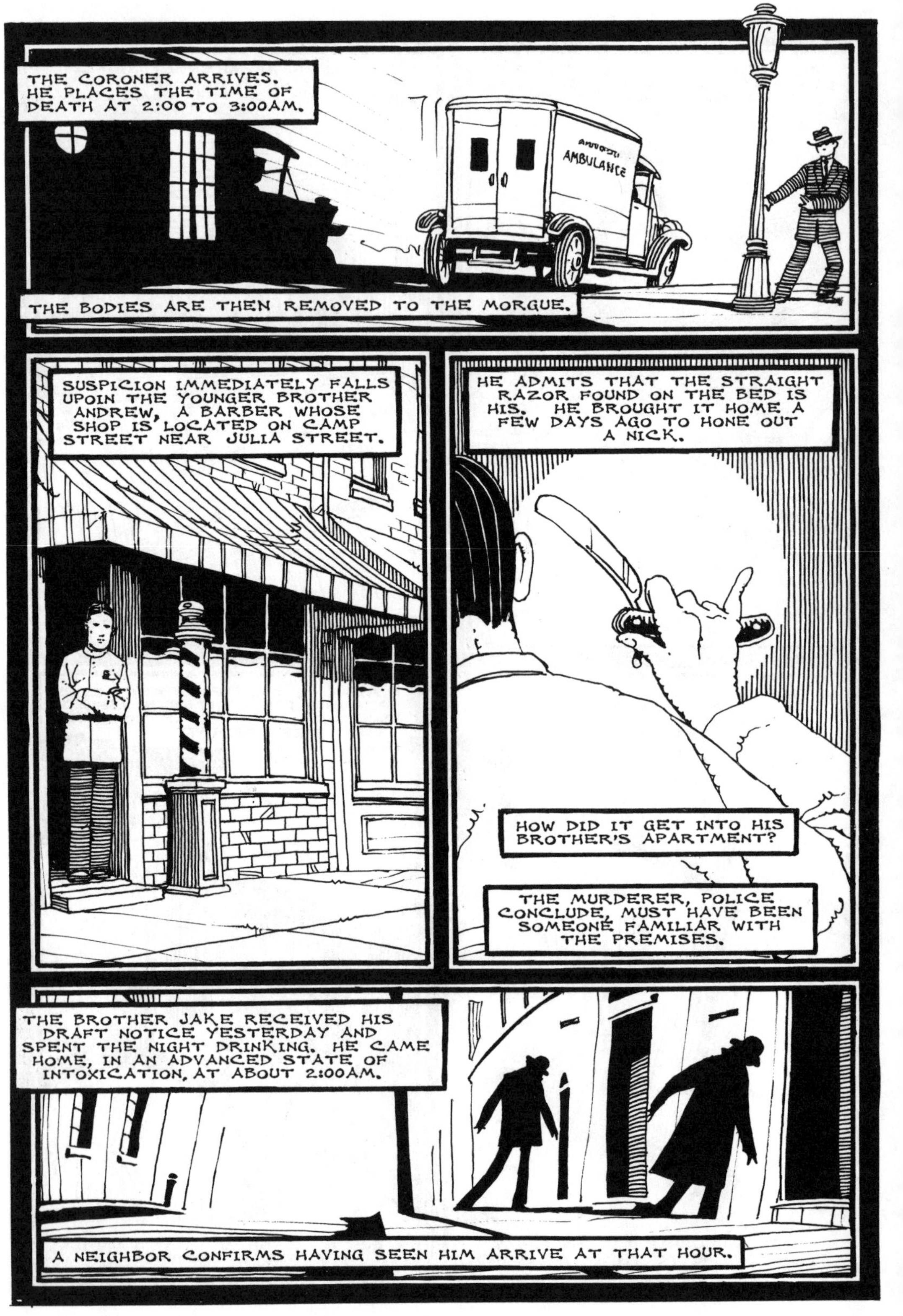
THE CORONER ARRIVES. HE PLACES THE TIME OF DEATH AT 2:00 TO 3:00AM.
AMBULANCE
THE BODIES ARE THEN REMOVED TO THE MORGUE.
SUSPICION IMMEDIATELY FALLS UPOIN THE YOUNGER BROTHER ANDREW, A BARBER WHOSE SHOP IS LOCATED ON CAMP STREET NEAR JULIA STREET.
HE ADMITS THAT THE STRAIGHT RAZOR FOUND ON THE BED IS HIS. HE BROUGHT IT HOME A FEW DAYS AGO TO HONE OUT A NICK.
HOW DID IT GET INTO HIS BROTHER'S APARTMENT?
THE MURDERER, POLICE CONCLUDE, MUST HAVE BEEN SOMEONE FAMILIAR WITH THE PREMISES.
THE BROTHER JAKE RECEIVED HIS DRAFT NOTICE YESTERDAY AND SPENT THE NIGHT DRINKING. HE CAME HOME, IN AN ADVANCED STATE OF INTOXICATION, AT ABOUT 2:00AM.
A NEIGHBOR CONFIRMS HAVING SEEN HIM ARRIVE AT THAT HOUR.

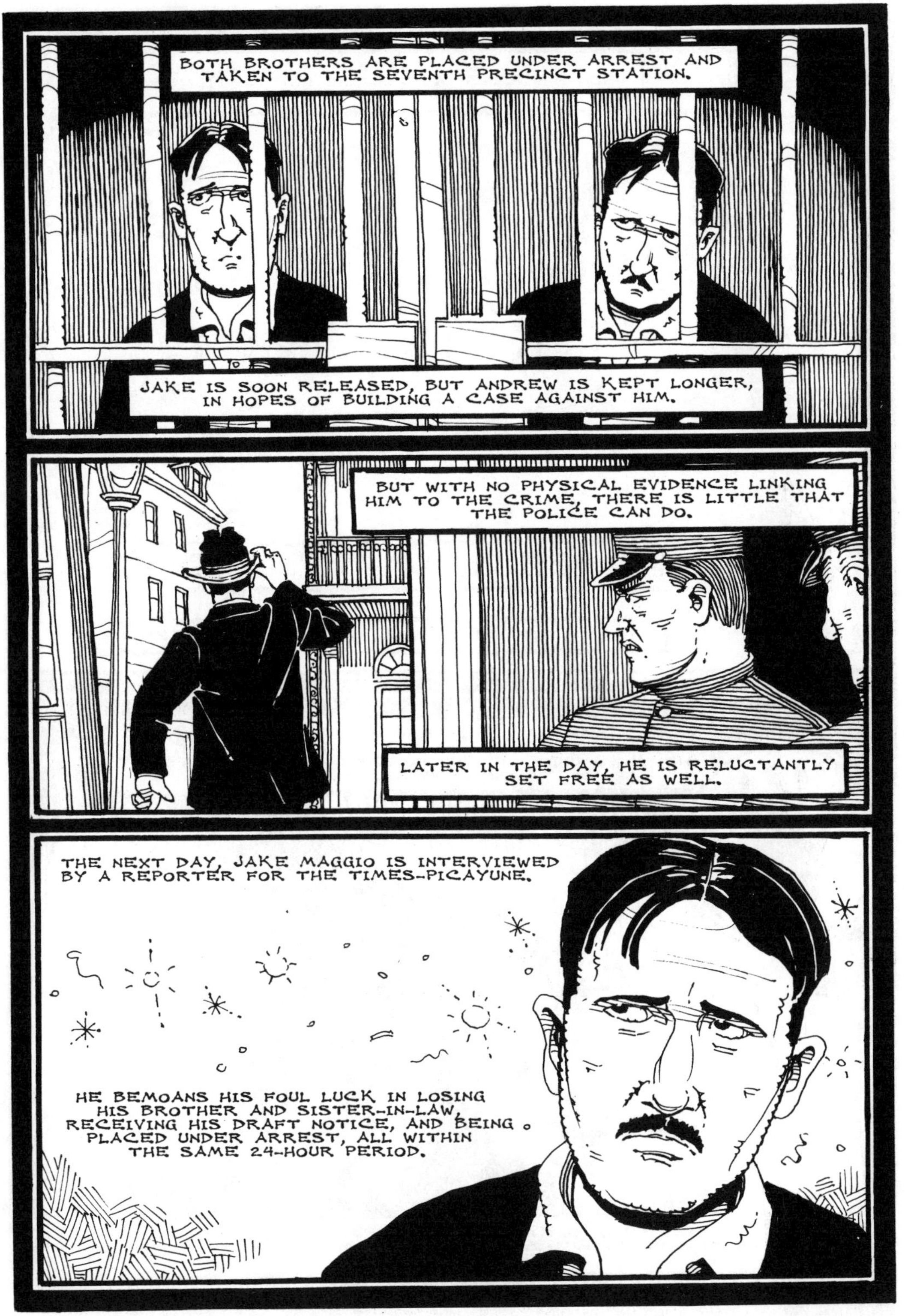
BOTH BROTHERS ARE PLACED UNDER ARREST AND TAKEN TO THE SEVENTH PRECINCT STATION.
JAKE IS SOON RELEASED, BUT ANDREW IS KEPT LONGER, IN HOPES OF BUILDING A CASE AGAINST HIM.
BUT WITH NO PHYSICAL EVIDENCE LINKING HIM TO THE CRIME, THERE IS LITTLE THAT THE POLICE CAN DO.
LATER IN THE DAY, HE IS RELUCTANTLY SET FREE AS WELL.
THE NEXT DAY, JAKE MAGGIO IS INTERVIEWED BY A REPORTER FOR THE TIMES-PICAYUNE.
HE BEMOANS HIS FOUL LUCK IN LOSING HIS BROTHER AND SISTER-IN-LAW, RECEIVING HIS DRAFT NOTICE, AND BEING PLACED UNDER ARREST, ALL WITHIN THE SAME 24-HOUR PERIOD.

ONE BLOCK FROM THE MURDER SCENE, AT UPPERLINE AND ROBERTSON STREETS, A PUZZLING INSCRIPTION IS FOUND SCRAWLED IN CHALK ON THE SIDEWALK.

MRS MAGGIO IS GOING TO SIT UP TONIGHT JUST LIKE MRS TONEY

IS THIS A CHILDISH PRANK? A MESSAGE LEFT BY THE KILLER? A WARNING LEFT BY AN ACCOMPLICE?

WAS IT WRITTEN BEFORE OR AFTER THE DEED?

MANY OBSERVERS, INCLUDING POLICE OFFICERS, SEE IN THIS THE WORK OF THE BLACK HAND, THE INFAMOUS UNDERGROUND FORCE THAT PREYS UPON ITALIAN IMMIGRANTS.

WHO IS "MRS. TONEY?" THE NAME PUTS SOME PEOPLE IN MIND OF A SERIES OF CRIMES COMMITTED SEVERAL YEARS AGO ...

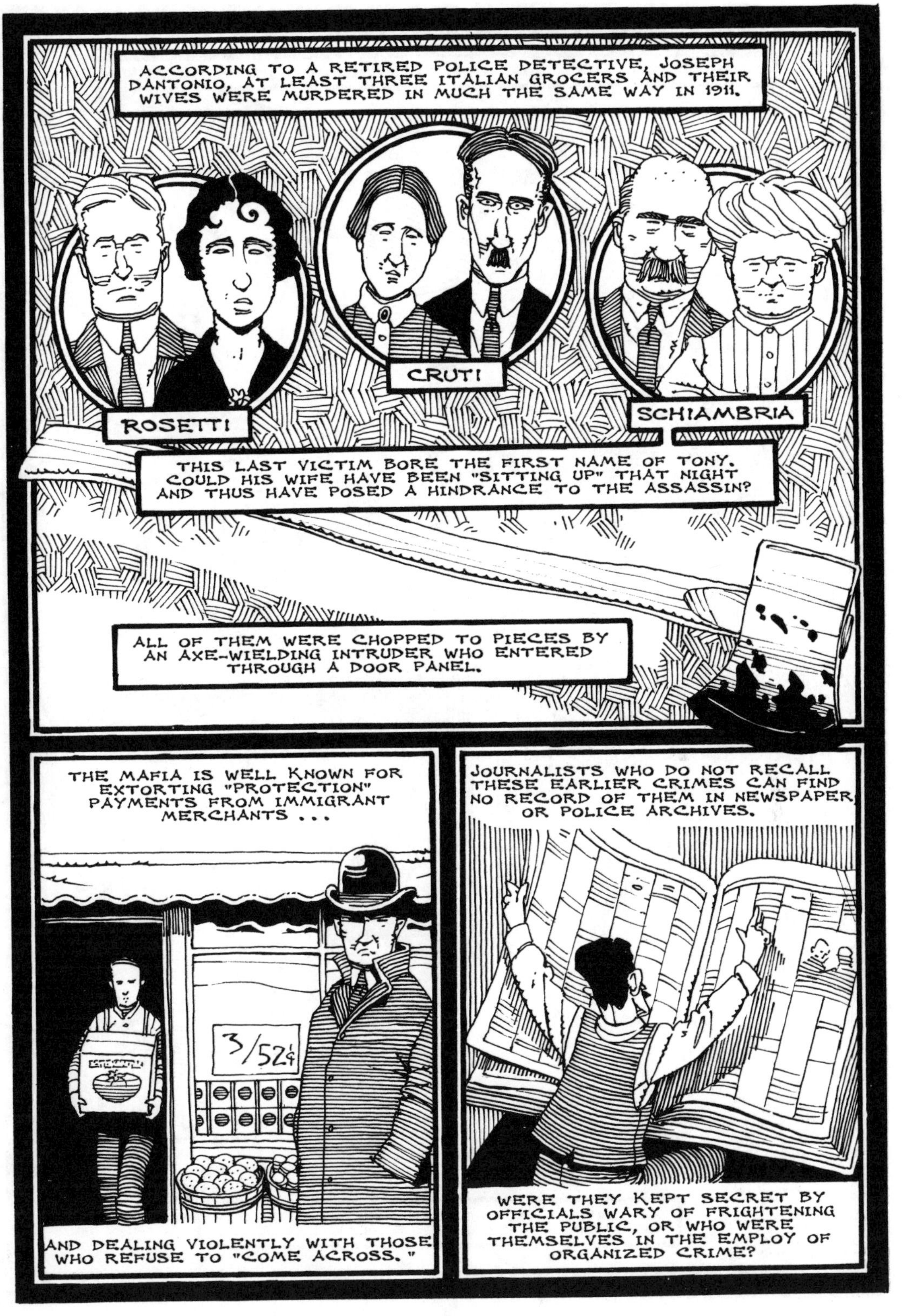
ACCORDING TO A RETIRED POLICE DETECTIVE, JOSEPH DANTONIO, AT LEAST THREE ITALIAN GROCERS AND THEIR WIVES WERE MURDERED IN MUCH THE SAME WAY IN 1911.
ROSETTI
CRUTI
SCHIAMBRIA
THIS LAST VICTIM BORE THE FIRST NAME OF TONY. COULD HIS WIFE HAVE BEEN "SITTING UP" THAT NIGHT AND THUS HAVE POSED A HINDRANCE TO THE ASSASSIN?
ALL OF THEM WERE CHOPPED TO PIECES BY AN AXE-WIELDING INTRUDER WHO ENTERED THROUGH A DOOR PANEL.
THE MAFIA IS WELL KNOWN FOR EXTORTING "PROTECTION" PAYMENTS FROM IMMIGRANT MERCHANTS ...
3/52¢
AND DEALING VIOLENTLY WITH THOSE WHO REFUSE TO "COME ACROSS."
JOURNALISTS WHO DO NOT RECALL THESE EARLIER CRIMES CAN FIND NO RECORD OF THEM IN NEWSPAPER OR POLICE ARCHIVES.
WERE THEY KEPT SECRET BY OFFICIALS WARY OF FRIGHTENING THE PUBLIC, OR WHO WERE THEMSELVES IN THE EMPLOY OF ORGANIZED CRIME?

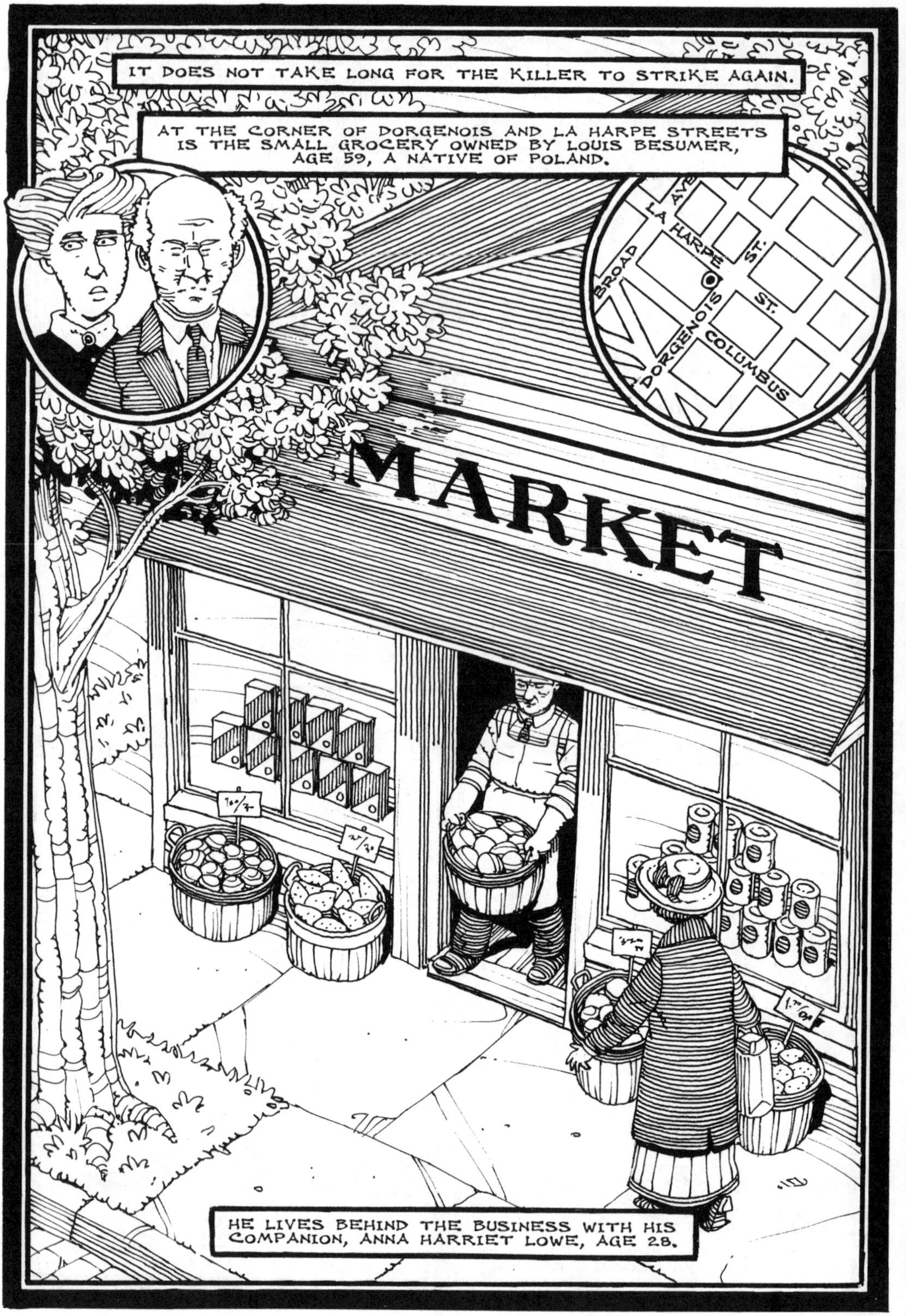
IT DOES NOT TAKE LONG FOR THE KILLER TO STRIKE AGAIN.
AT THE CORNER OF DORGENOIS AND LA HARPE STREETS IS THE SMALL GROCERY OWNED BY LOUIS BESUMER, AGE 59, A NATIVE OF POLAND.
LA HARPE
AVE
ST.
BROAD
DORGENOIS
ST.
COLUMBUS
MARKET
HE LIVES BEHIND THE BUSINESS WITH HIS COMPANION, ANNA HARRIET LOWE, AGE 28.

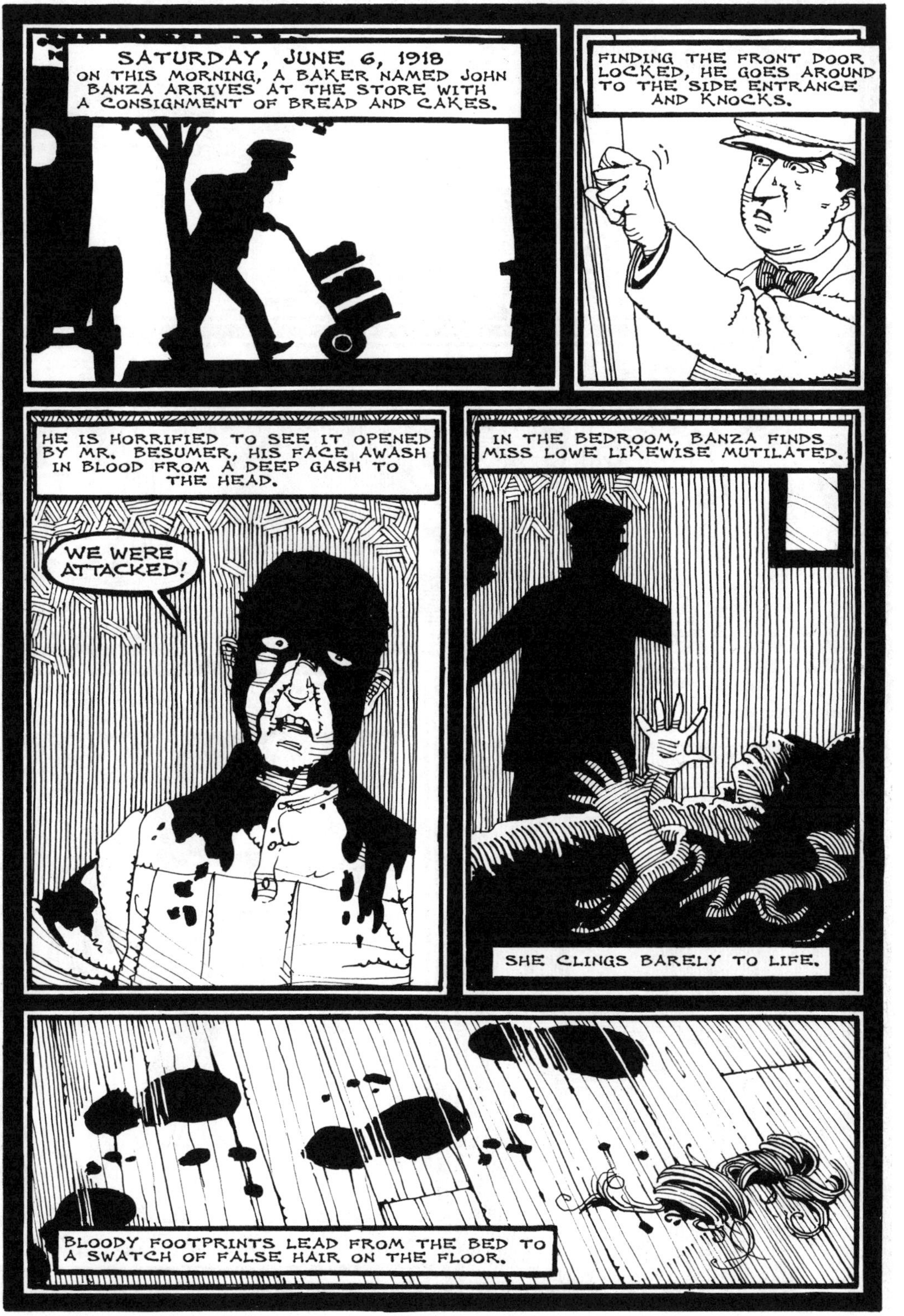
SATURDAY, JUNE 6, 1918
ON THIS MORNING, A BAKER NAMED JOHN BANZA ARRIVES AT THE STORE WITH A CONSIGNMENT OF BREAD AND CAKES.
FINDING THE FRONT DOOR LOCKED, HE GOES AROUND TO THE SIDE ENTRANCE AND KNOCKS.
HE IS HORRIFIED TO SEE IT OPENED BY MR. BESUMER, HIS FACE AWASH IN BLOOD FROM A DEEP GASH TO THE HEAD.
WE WERE ATTACKED!
IN THE BEDROOM, BANZA FINDS MISS LOWE LIKEWISE MUTILATED.
SHE CLINGS BARELY TO LIFE.
BLOODY FOOTPRINTS LEAD FROM THE BED TO A SWATCH OF FALSE HAIR ON THE FLOOR.

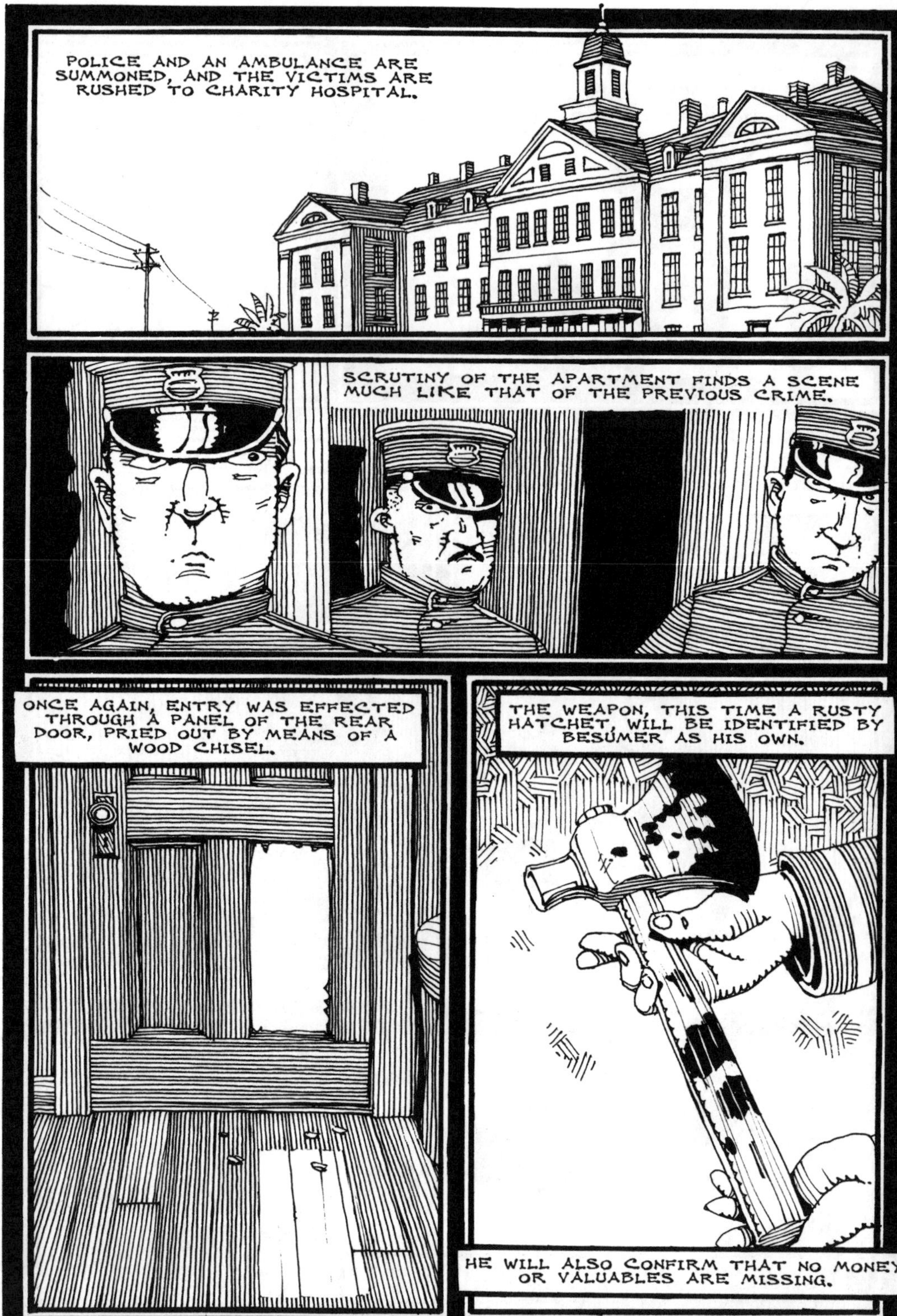
POLICE AND AN AMBULANCE ARE SUMMONED, AND THE VICTIMS ARE RUSHED TO CHARITY HOSPITAL.
SCRUTINY OF THE APARTMENT FINDS A SCENE MUCH LIKE THAT OF THE PREVIOUS CRIME.
ONCE AGAIN, ENTRY WAS EFFECTED THROUGH A PANEL OF THE REAR DOOR, PRIED OUT BY MEANS OF A WOOD CHISEL.
THE WEAPON, THIS TIME A RUSTY HATCHET, WILL BE IDENTIFIED BY BESUMER AS HIS OWN.
HE WILL ALSO CONFIRM THAT NO MONEY OR VALUABLES ARE MISSING.

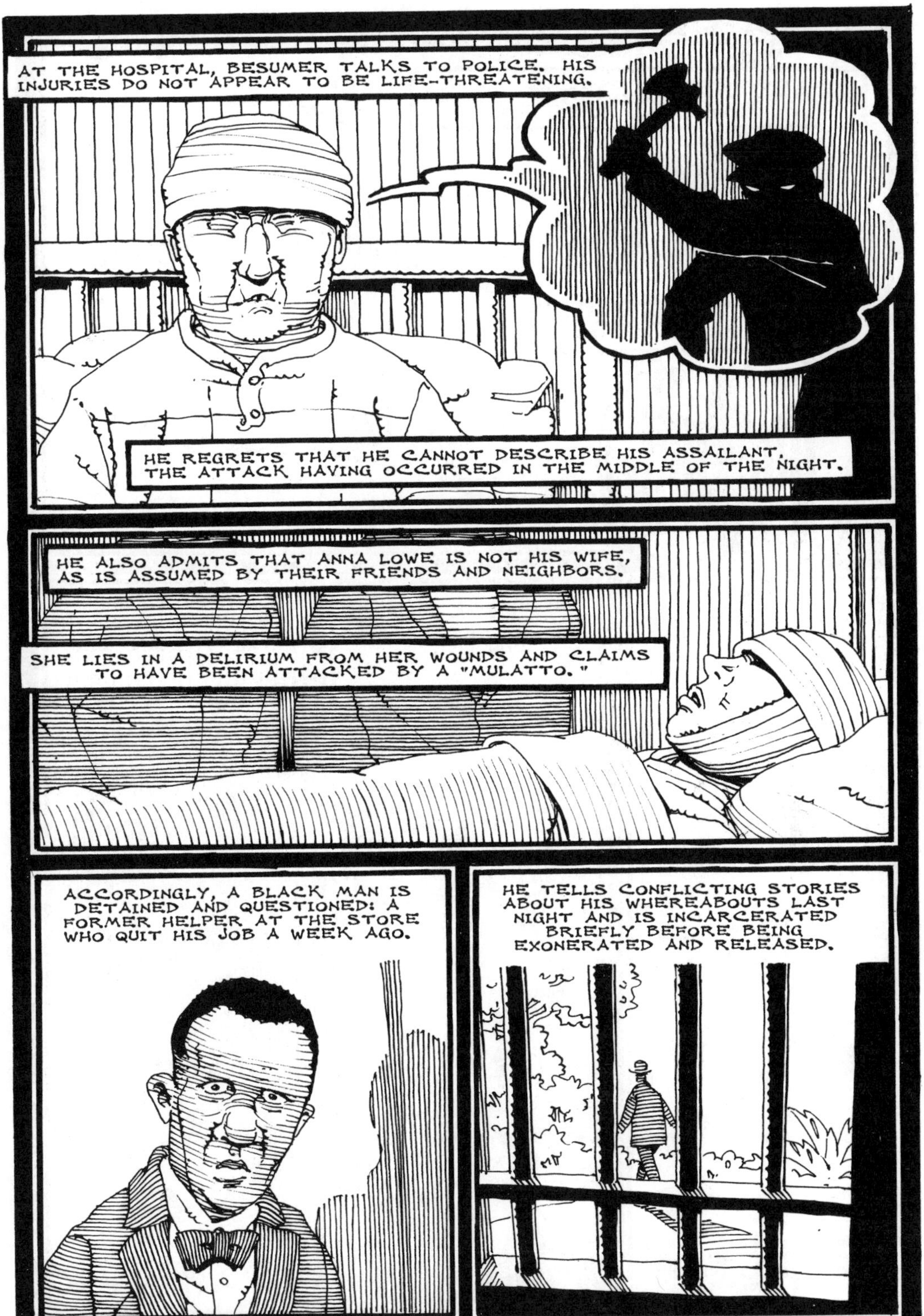
AT THE HOSPITAL, BESUMER TALKS TO POLICE. HIS INJURIES DO NOT APPEAR TO BE LIFE-THREATENING.
HE REGRETS THAT HE CANNOT DESCRIBE HIS ASSAILANT, THE ATTACK HAVING OCCURRED IN THE MIDDLE OF THE NIGHT.
HE ALSO ADMITS THAT ANNA LOWE IS NOT HIS WIFE, AS IS ASSUMED BY THEIR FRIENDS AND NEIGHBORS.
SHE LIES IN A DELIRIUM FROM HER WOUNDS AND CLAIMS TO HAVE BEEN ATTACKED BY A "MULATTO."
ACCORDINGLY, A BLACK MAN IS DETAINED AND QUESTIONED: A FORMER HELPER AT THE STORE WHO QUIT HIS JOB A WEEK AGO.
HE TELLS CONFLICTING STORIES ABOUT HIS WHEREABOUTS LAST NIGHT AND IS INCARCERATED BRIEFLY BEFORE BEING EXONERATED AND RELEASED.

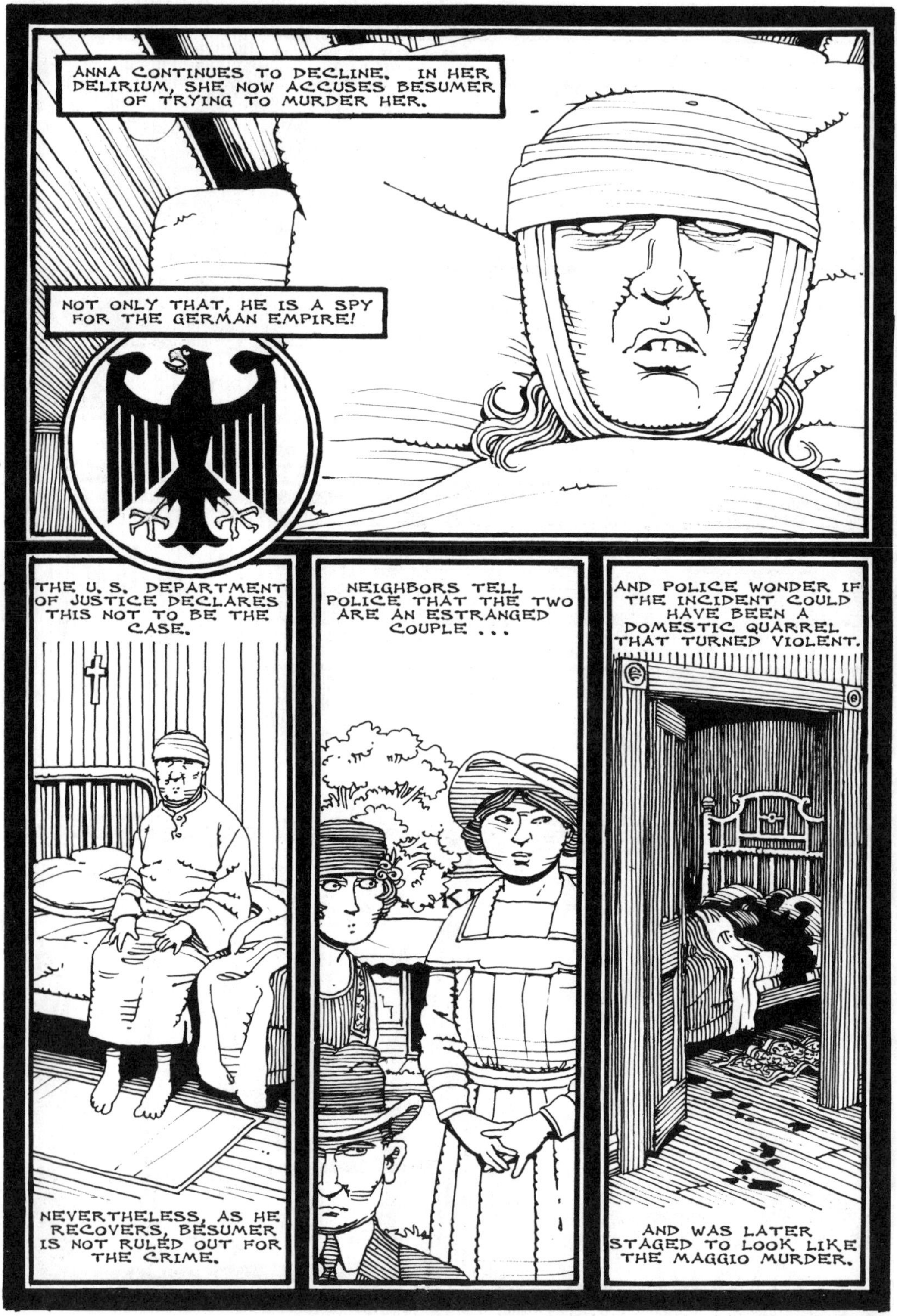
ANNA CONTINUES TO DECLINE. IN HER DELIRIUM, SHE NOW ACCUSES BESUMER OF TRYING TO MURDER HER.
NOT ONLY THAT, HE IS A SPY FOR THE GERMAN EMPIRE!
THE U.S. DEPARTMENT OF JUSTICE DECLARES THIS NOT TO BE THE CASE.
NEVERTHELESS, AS HE RECOVERS, BESUMER IS NOT RULED OUT FOR THE CRIME.
NEIGHBORS TELL POLICE THAT THE TWO ARE AN ESTRANGED COUPLE ...
AND POLICE WONDER IF THE INCIDENT COULD HAVE BEEN A DOMESTIC QUARREL THAT TURNED VIOLENT.
AND WAS LATER STAGED TO LOOK LIKE THE MAGGIO MURDER.

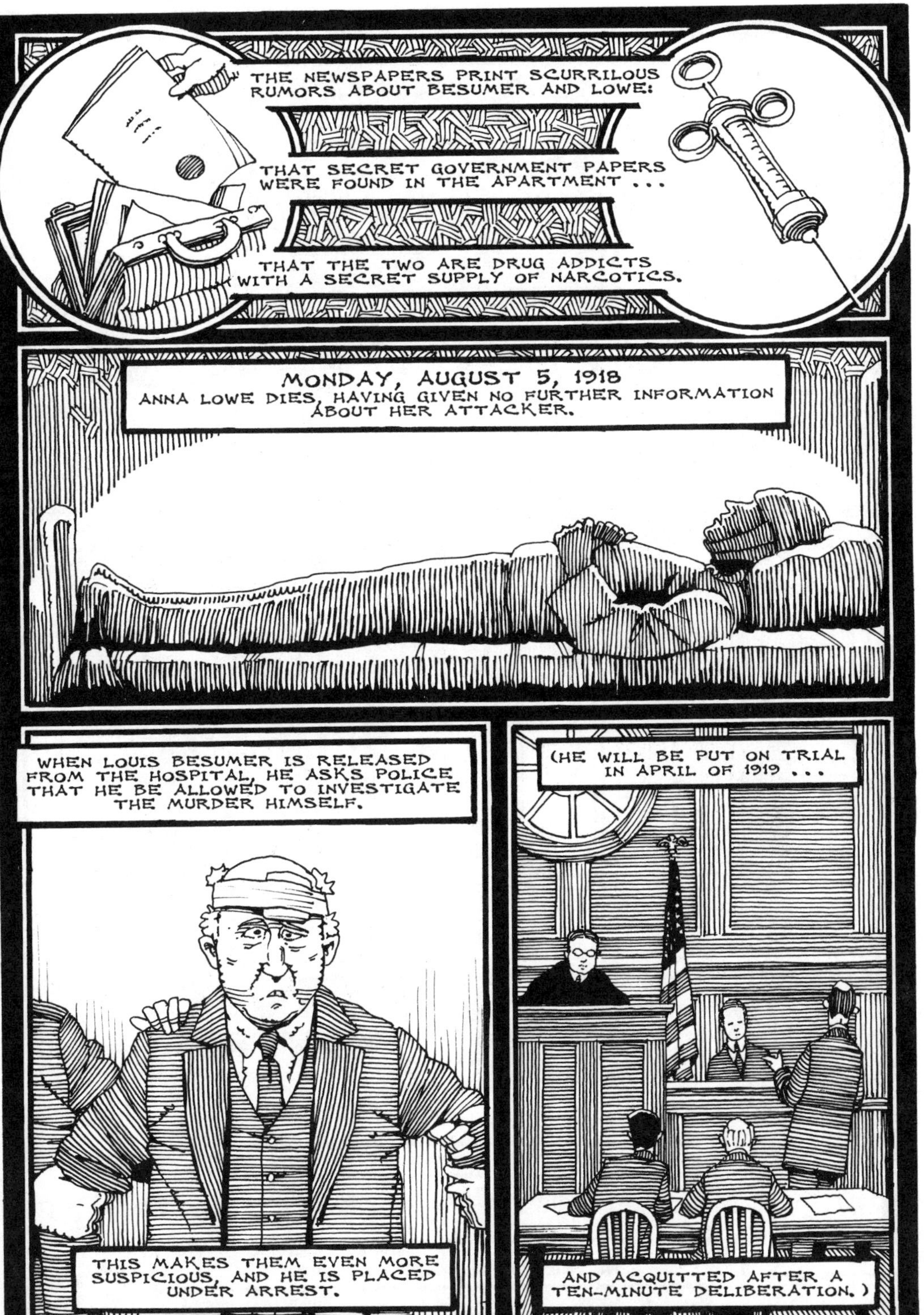
THE NEWSPAPERS PRINT SCURRILOUS RUMORS ABOUT BESUMER AND LOWE:
THAT SECRET GOVERNMENT PAPERS WERE FOUND IN THE APARTMENT . . .
THAT THE TWO ARE DRUG ADDICTS WITH A SECRET SUPPLY OF NARCOTICS.
MONDAY, AUGUST 5, 1918
ANNA LOWE DIES, HAVING GIVEN NO FURTHER INFORMATION ABOUT HER ATTACKER.
WHEN LOUIS BESUMER IS RELEASED FROM THE HOSPITAL, HE ASKS POLICE THAT HE BE ALLOWED TO INVESTIGATE THE MURDER HIMSELF.
THIS MAKES THEM EVEN MORE SUSPICIOUS, AND HE IS PLACED UNDER ARREST.
(HE WILL BE PUT ON TRIAL IN APRIL OF 1919 . . .
AND ACQUITTED AFTER A TEN-MINUTE DELIBERATION.)

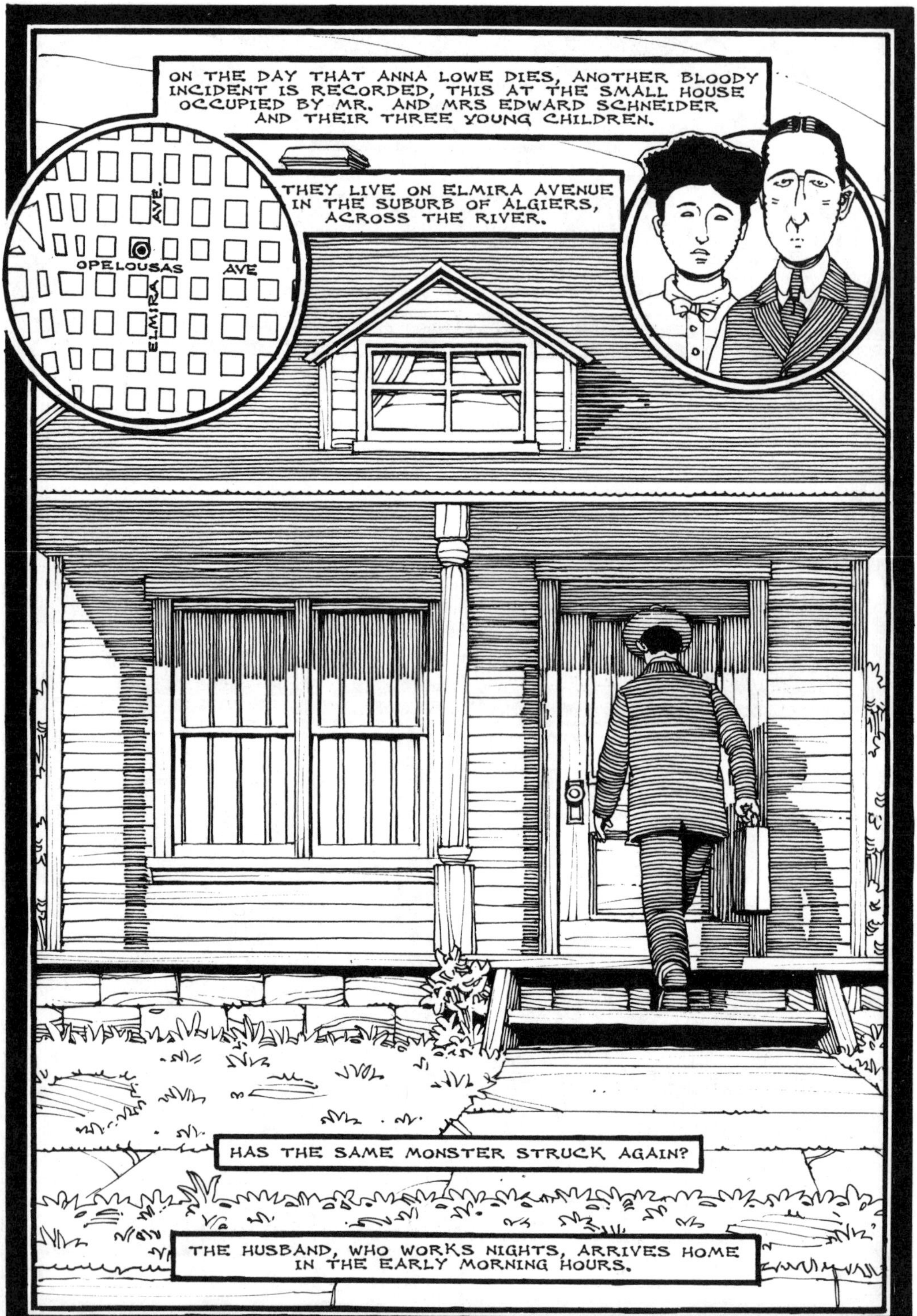
ON THE DAY THAT ANNA LOWE DIES, ANOTHER BLOODY INCIDENT IS RECORDED, THIS AT THE SMALL HOUSE OCCUPIED BY MR. AND MRS EDWARD SCHNEIDER AND THEIR THREE YOUNG CHILDREN.
ELMIRA AVE.
OPELOUSAS AVE
THEY LIVE ON ELMIRA AVENUE IN THE SUBURB OF ALGIERS, ACROSS THE RIVER.
HAS THE SAME MONSTER STRUCK AGAIN?
THE HUSBAND, WHO WORKS NIGHTS, ARRIVES HOME IN THE EARLY MORNING HOURS.

UPON ENTERING THE HOUSE, HE SENSES AN UNUSUAL ATMOSPHERE. THE PLACE IS TOO QUIET.

HE CALLS OUT TO HIS WIFE, WHO IS IN HER EIGHTH MONTH OF PREGNANCY, BUT RECEIVES NO RESPONSE.

HE FINDS HER LYING ON THEIR BED, BLEEDING PROFUSELY FROM SEVERAL CUTS TO THE HEAD --- BUT STILL ALIVE.

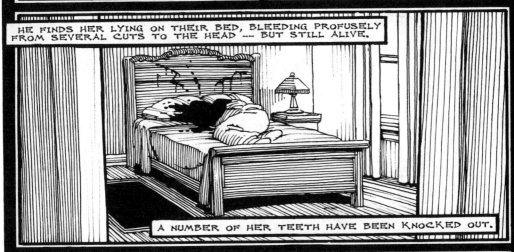

A NUMBER OF HER TEETH HAVE BEEN KNOCKED OUT.

POLICE AND AN AMBULANCE ARE CALLED AT ONCE.

AN EXAMINATION OF THE SCENE, HOWEVER, FINDS LITTLE THAT CONNECTS IT TO THE PREVIOUS CRIMES.

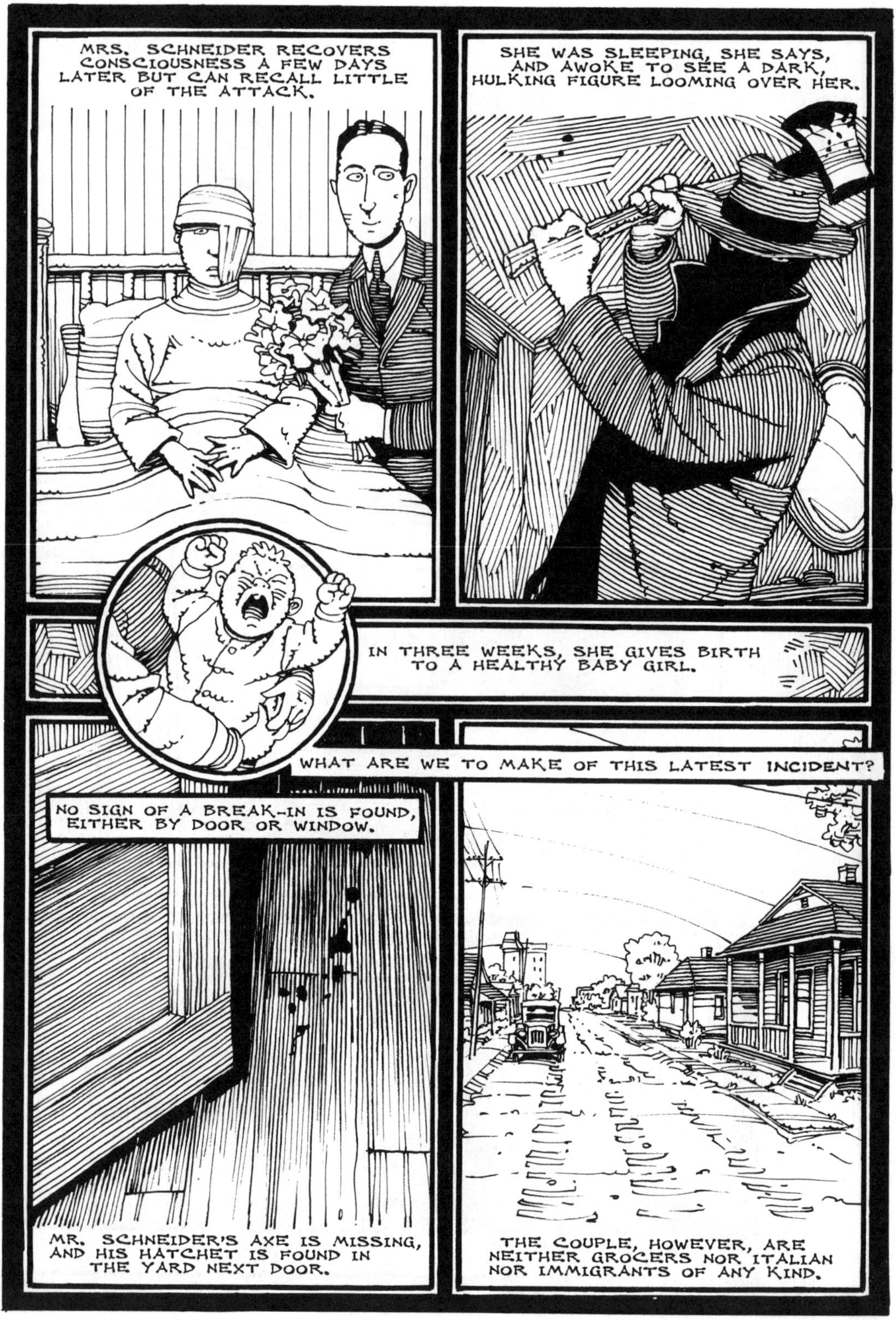
MRS. SCHNEIDER RECOVERS CONSCIOUSNESS A FEW DAYS LATER BUT CAN RECALL LITTLE OF THE ATTACK.
SHE WAS SLEEPING, SHE SAYS, AND AWOKE TO SEE A DARK, HULKING FIGURE LOOMING OVER HER.
IN THREE WEEKS, SHE GIVES BIRTH TO A HEALTHY BABY GIRL.
NO SIGN OF A BREAK-IN IS FOUND, EITHER BY DOOR OR WINDOW.
MR. SCHNEIDER'S AXE IS MISSING, AND HIS HATCHET IS FOUND IN THE YARD NEXT DOOR.
WHAT ARE WE TO MAKE OF THIS LATEST INCIDENT?
THE COUPLE, HOWEVER, ARE NEITHER GROCERS NOR ITALIAN NOR IMMIGRANTS OF ANY KIND.

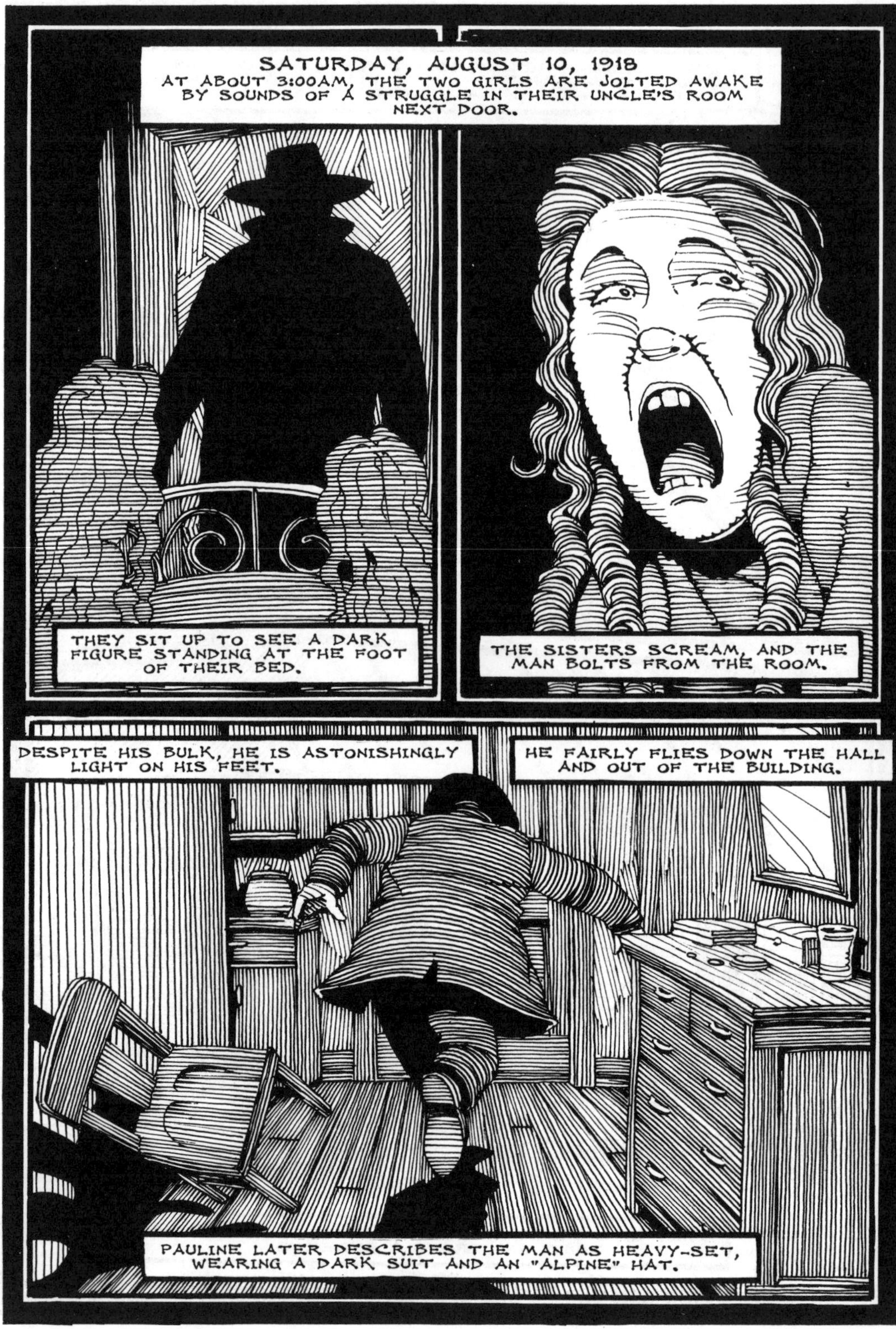
SATURDAY, AUGUST 10, 1918
AT ABOUT 3:00AM, THE TWO GIRLS ARE JOLTED AWAKE BY SOUNDS OF A STRUGGLE IN THEIR UNCLE'S ROOM NEXT DOOR.
THEY SIT UP TO SEE A DARK FIGURE STANDING AT THE FOOT OF THEIR BED.
THE SISTERS SCREAM, AND THE MAN BOLTS FROM THE ROOM.
DESPITE HIS BULK, HE IS ASTONISHINGLY LIGHT ON HIS FEET.
HE FAIRLY FLIES DOWN THE HALL AND OUT OF THE BUILDING.
PAULINE LATER DESCRIBES THE MAN AS HEAVY-SET, WEARING A DARK SUIT AND AN "ALPINE" HAT.

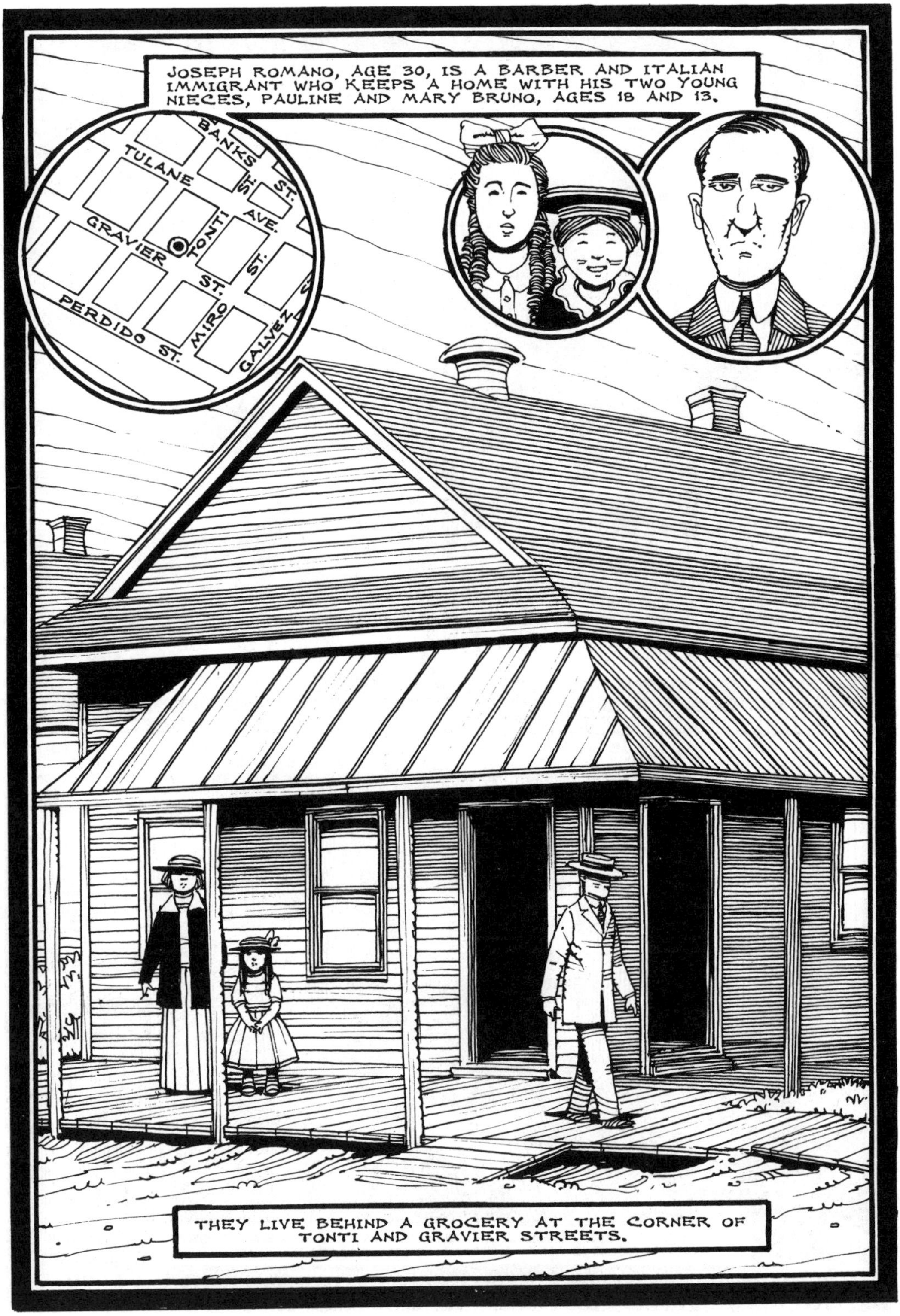
JOSEPH ROMANO, AGE 30, IS A BARBER AND ITALIAN IMMIGRANT WHO KEEPS A HOME WITH HIS TWO YOUNG NIECES, PAULINE AND MARY BRUNO, AGES 18 AND 13.
BANKS ST.
TULANE AVE.
GRAVIER ST.
TONTI ST.
PERDIDO ST.
MIRO ST.
GALVEZ
THEY LIVE BEHIND A GROCERY AT THE CORNER OF TONTI AND GRAVIER STREETS.

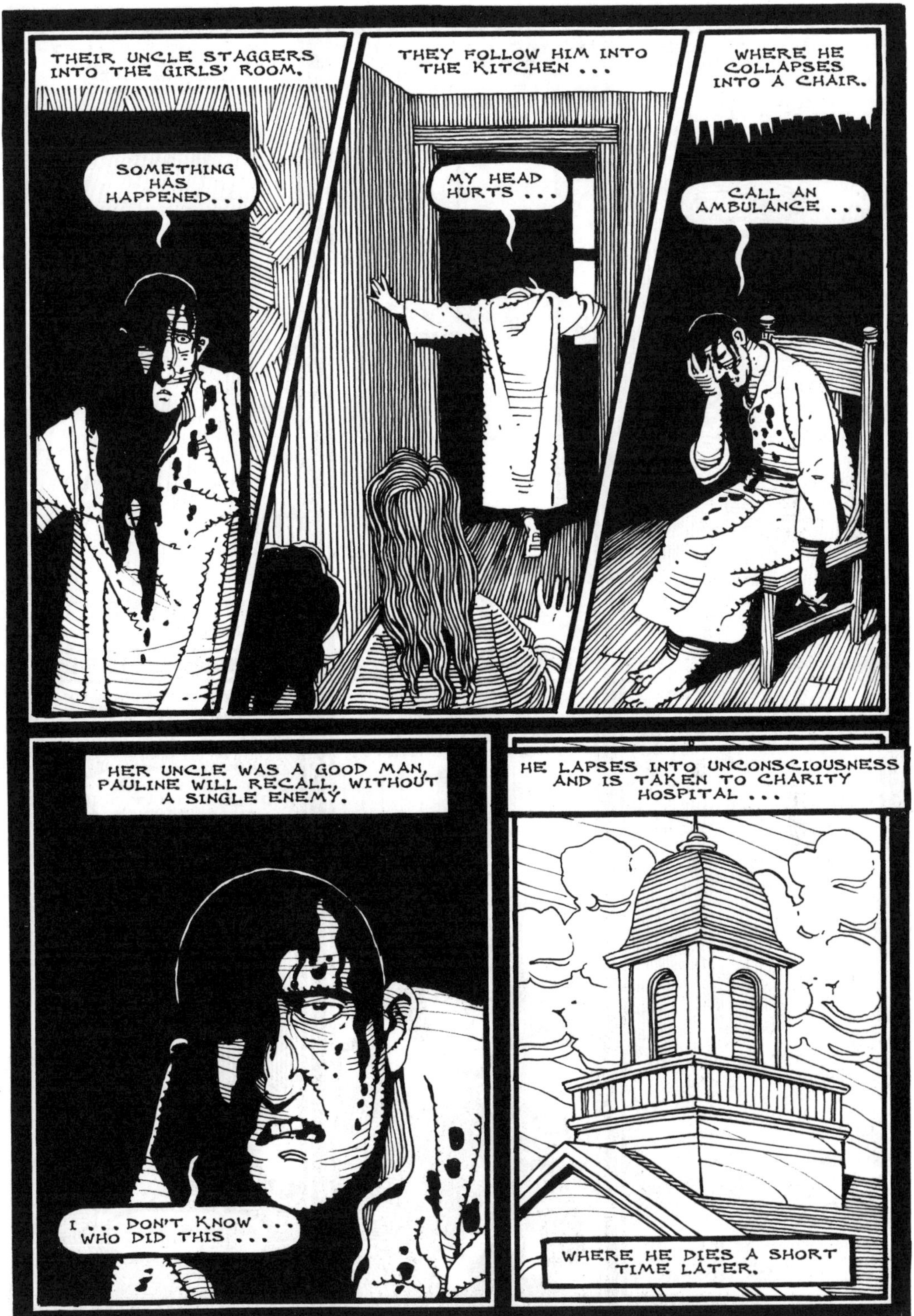
THEIR UNCLE STAGGERS INTO THE GIRLS' ROOM.
SOMETHING HAS HAPPENED...
THEY FOLLOW HIM INTO THE KITCHEN ...
MY HEAD HURTS ...
WHERE HE COLLAPSES INTO A CHAIR.
CALL AN AMBULANCE ...
HER UNCLE WAS A GOOD MAN, PAULINE WILL RECALL, WITHOUT A SINGLE ENEMY.
I ... DON'T KNOW ... WHO DID THIS ...
HE LAPSES INTO UNCONSCIOUSNESS AND IS TAKEN TO CHARITY HOSPITAL ...
WHERE HE DIES A SHORT TIME LATER.

THE FIRST POLICEMAN ON THE SCENE IS PATROLMAN CHISHOLM OF THE FIRST PRECINCT STATION, JUST TWO BLOCKS AWAY.

HE IS ALERTED BY THE SCREAMS OF THE BRUNO GIRLS.

POLICE SURMISE THAT THE KILLER LEAPT THE FENCE FROM THE ALLEY BEHIND THE BUILDING ...

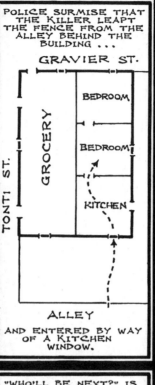

GRAVIER ST.

TONTI ST.

GROCERY

BEDROOM

BEDROOM

KITCHEN

ALLEY

AND ENTERED BY WAY OF A KITCHEN WINDOW.

THE BLOOD-SMEARED MURDER WEAPON IS FOUND ON THE KITCHEN FLOOR.

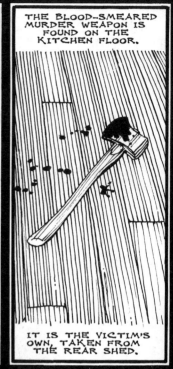

IT IS THE VICTIM'S OWN, TAKEN FROM THE REAR SHED.

HIS ROOM IS TORN APART FROM HIS STRUGGLE WITH THE ASSASSIN, BUT THERE APPEARS TO HAVE BEEN NO ROBBERY.

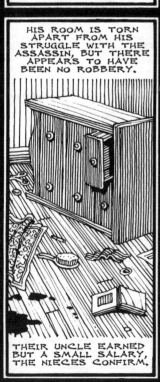

THEIR UNCLE EARNED BUT A SMALL SALARY, THE NIECES CONFIRM.

"WHO'LL BE NEXT?" IS THE QUESTION CIRCULATING THROUGH THE TERRIFIED ITALIAN COMMUNITY.

SUPERINTENDENT OF POLICE MOONEY DECLARES:

I AM OF THE BELIEF THAT THE MURDERER IS A DEPRAVED CRIMINAL WITH NO REGARD FOR HUMAN LIFE ...

AND WE WILL GET HIM!

PART III

A CITY IN TERROR

WITH THEIR CITY FLOWING RED, CITIZENS GIVE WAY TO NERVOUSNESS AND PANIC.

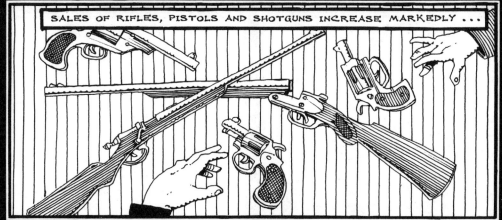

SALES OF RIFLES, PISTOLS AND SHOTGUNS INCREASE MARKEDLY ...

AS DOES THE INSTALLATION OF BARS, GRATES AND GRILLES.

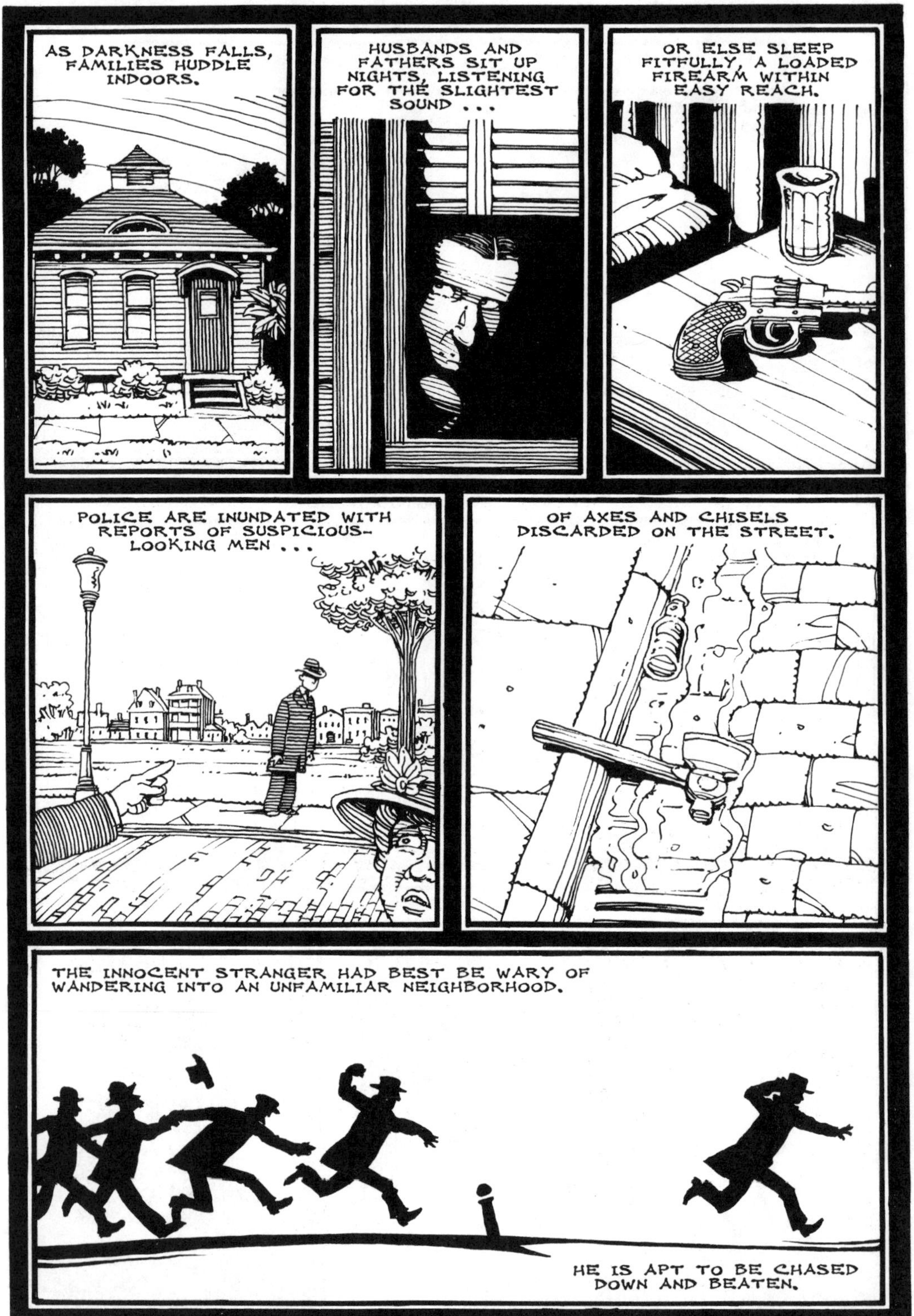
AS DARKNESS FALLS, FAMILIES HUDDLE INDOORS.
HUSBANDS AND FATHERS SIT UP NIGHTS, LISTENING FOR THE SLIGHTEST SOUND . . .
OR ELSE SLEEP FITFULLY, A LOADED FIREARM WITHIN EASY REACH.
POLICE ARE INUNDATED WITH REPORTS OF SUSPICIOUS-LOOKING MEN . . .
OF AXES AND CHISELS DISCARDED ON THE STREET.
THE INNOCENT STRANGER HAD BEST BE WARY OF WANDERING INTO AN UNFAMILIAR NEIGHBORHOOD.
HE IS APT TO BE CHASED DOWN AND BEATEN.

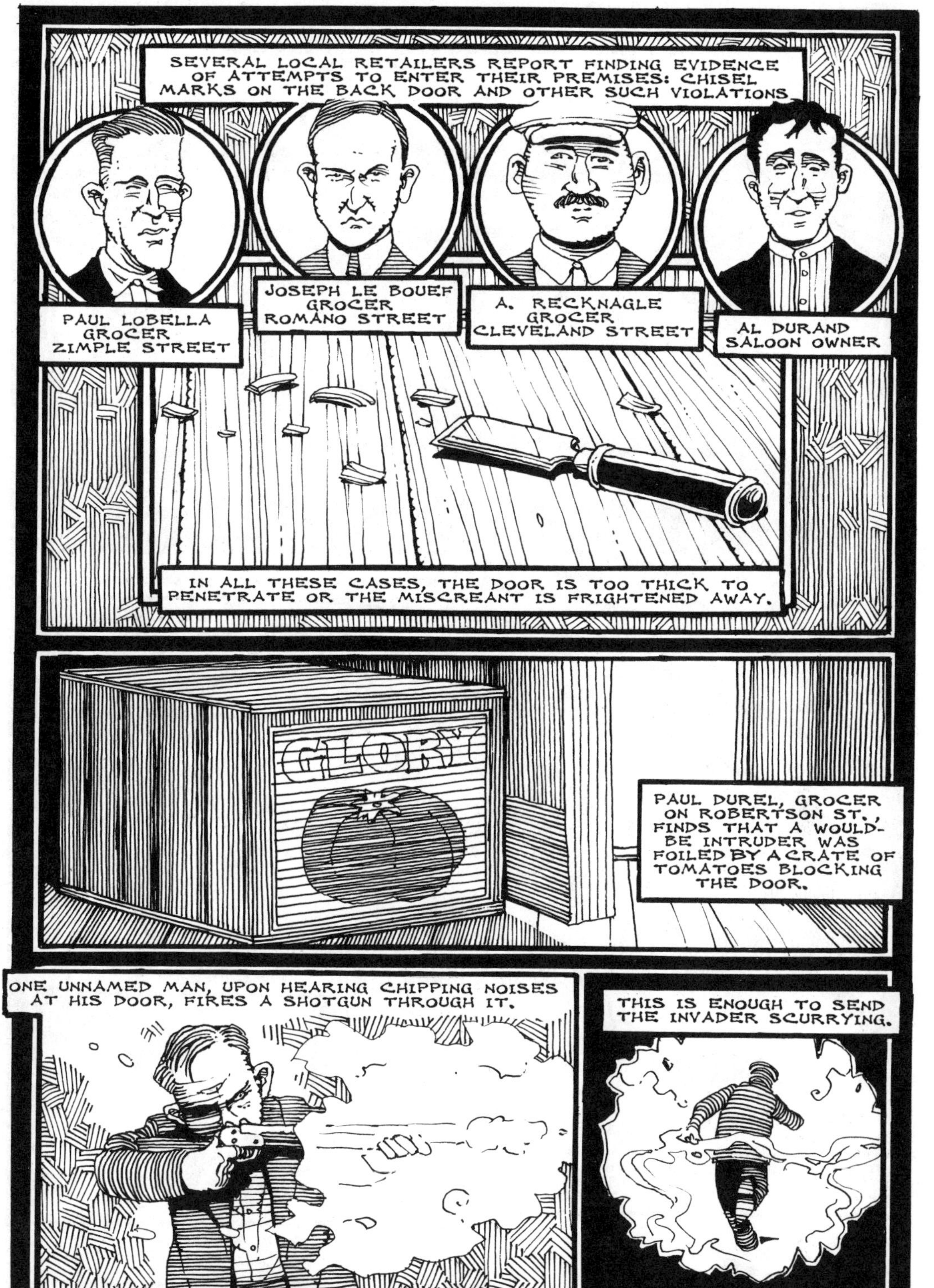
SEVERAL LOCAL RETAILERS REPORT FINDING EVIDENCE OF ATTEMPTS TO ENTER THEIR PREMISES: CHISEL MARKS ON THE BACK DOOR AND OTHER SUCH VIOLATIONS.
PAUL LOBELLA GROCER ZIMPLE STREET
JOSEPH LE BOUEF GROCER ROMANO STREET
A. RECKNAGLE GROCER CLEVELAND STREET
AL DURAND SALOON OWNER
IN ALL THESE CASES, THE DOOR IS TOO THICK TO PENETRATE OR THE MISCREANT IS FRIGHTENED AWAY.
GLORY
PAUL DUREL, GROCER ON ROBERTSON ST., FINDS THAT A WOULD-BE INTRUDER WAS FOILED BY A CRATE OF TOMATOES BLOCKING THE DOOR.
ONE UNNAMED MAN, UPON HEARING CHIPPING NOISES AT HIS DOOR, FIRES A SHOTGUN THROUGH IT.
THIS IS ENOUGH TO SEND THE INVADER SCURRYING.

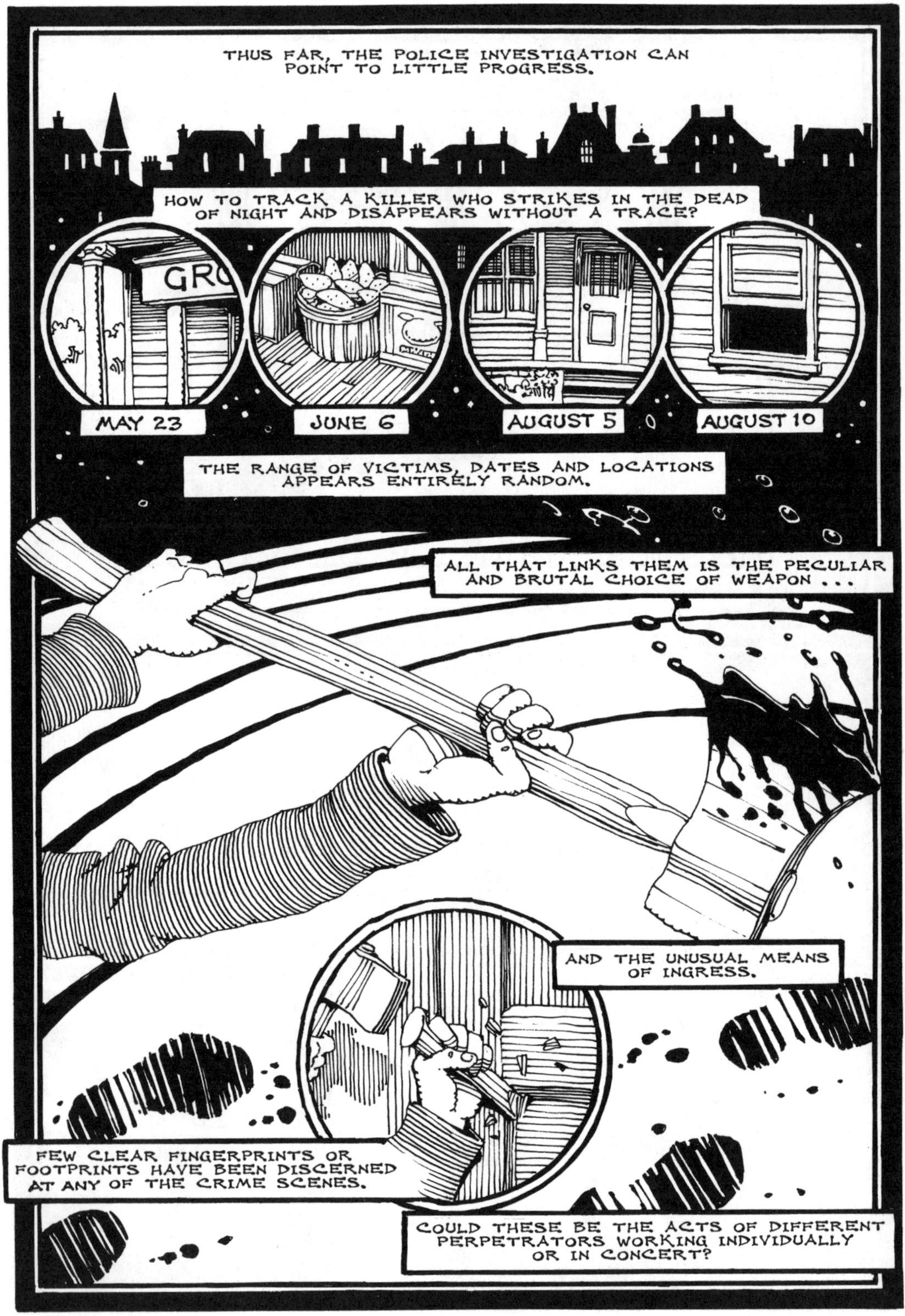
THUS FAR, THE POLICE INVESTIGATION CAN POINT TO LITTLE PROGRESS.
HOW TO TRACK A KILLER WHO STRIKES IN THE DEAD OF NIGHT AND DISAPPEARS WITHOUT A TRACE?
GRO
MAY 23
JUNE 6
AUGUST 5
AUGUST 10
THE RANGE OF VICTIMS, DATES AND LOCATIONS APPEARS ENTIRELY RANDOM.
ALL THAT LINKS THEM IS THE PECULIAR AND BRUTAL CHOICE OF WEAPON . . .
AND THE UNUSUAL MEANS OF INGRESS.
FEW CLEAR FINGERPRINTS OR FOOTPRINTS HAVE BEEN DISCERNED AT ANY OF THE CRIME SCENES.
COULD THESE BE THE ACTS OF DIFFERENT PERPETRATORS WORKING INDIVIDUALLY OR IN CONCERT?

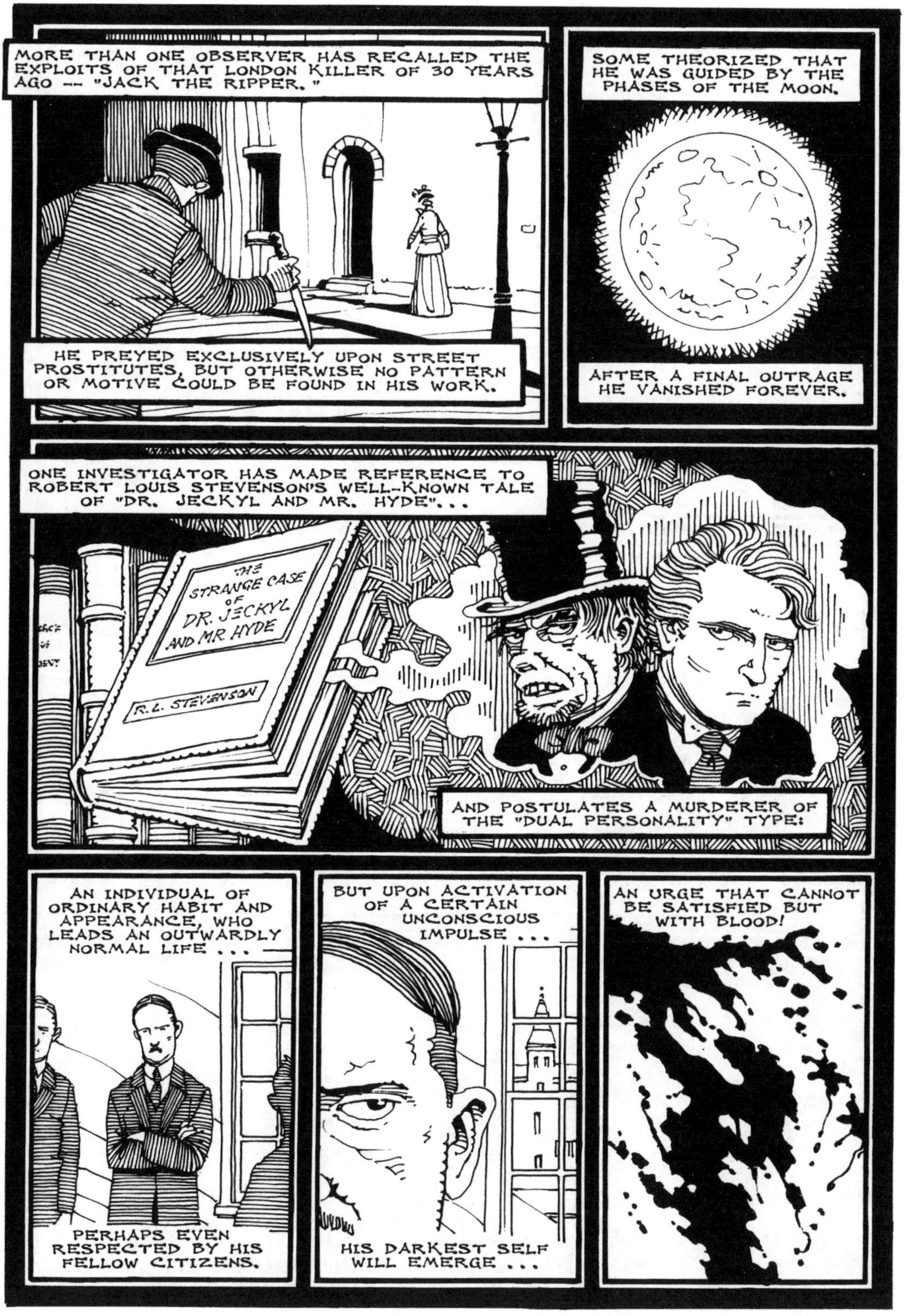
MORE THAN ONE OBSERVER HAS RECALLED THE EXPLOITS OF THAT LONDON KILLER OF 30 YEARS AGO -- "JACK THE RIPPER."
HE PREYED EXCLUSIVELY UPON STREET PROSTITUTES, BUT OTHERWISE NO PATTERN OR MOTIVE COULD BE FOUND IN HIS WORK.
SOME THEORIZED THAT HE WAS GUIDED BY THE PHASES OF THE MOON.
AFTER A FINAL OUTRAGE HE VANISHED FOREVER.
ONE INVESTIGATOR HAS MADE REFERENCE TO ROBERT LOUIS STEVENSON'S WELL-KNOWN TALE OF "DR. JECKYL AND MR. HYDE"...
THE STRANGE CASE OF DR. JECKYL AND MR HYDE
R.L. STEVENSON
AND POSTULATES A MURDERER OF THE "DUAL PERSONALITY" TYPE:
AN INDIVIDUAL OF ORDINARY HABIT AND APPEARANCE, WHO LEADS AN OUTWARDLY NORMAL LIFE ...
PERHAPS EVEN RESPECTED BY HIS FELLOW CITIZENS.
BUT UPON ACTIVATION OF A CERTAIN UNCONSCIOUS IMPULSE ...
HIS DARKEST SELF WILL EMERGE ...
AN URGE THAT CANNOT BE SATISFIED BUT WITH BLOOD!

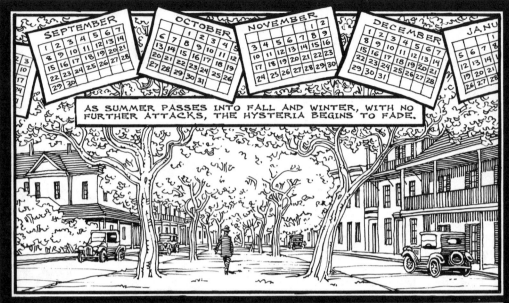

SEPTEMBER
OCTOBER
NOVEMBER
DECEMBER
JANU
AS SUMMER PASSES INTO FALL AND WINTER, WITH NO FURTHER ATTACKS, THE HYSTERIA BEGINS TO FADE.
THE WORLD WAR ENDS WITH THE ARMISTICE OF NOVEMBER 11.
THE CITY'S SOLDIERS ARRIVE HOME TO VICTORY PARADES AND WIDESPREAD CELEBRATION.
AS THE YEAR 1919 PROGRESSES, THE SAVAGE EVENTS OF THE PREVIOUS YEAR ARE FORGOTTEN . . .
ALMOST!

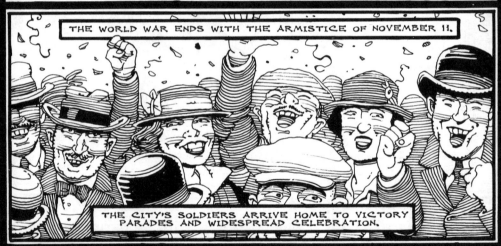

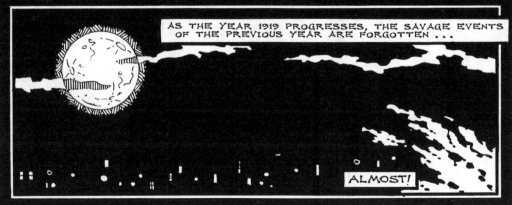

PART IV

JAZZ IT!

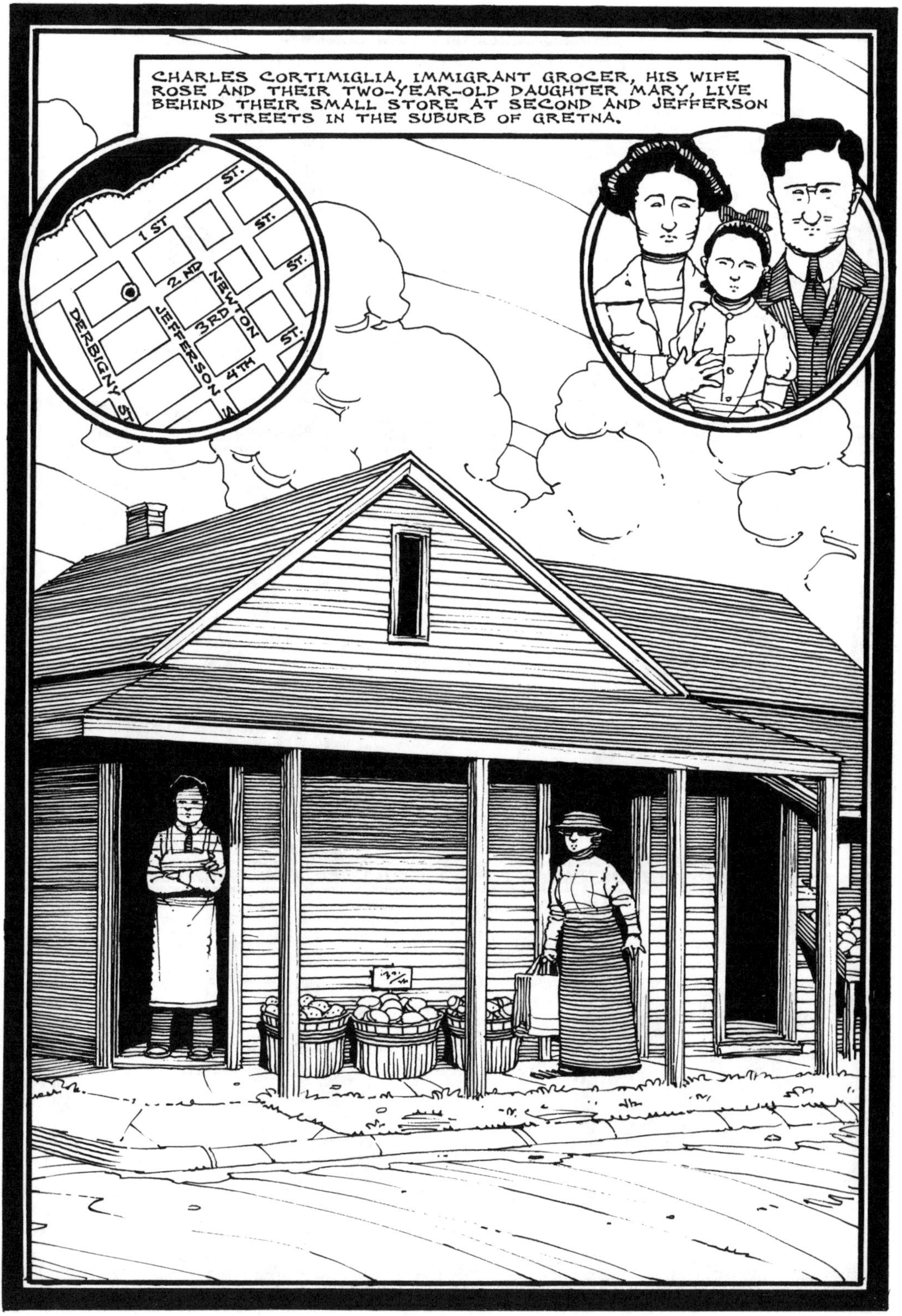
CHARLES CORTIMIGLIA, IMMIGRANT GROCER, HIS WIFE ROSE AND THEIR TWO-YEAR-OLD DAUGHTER MARY, LIVE BEHIND THEIR SMALL STORE AT SECOND AND JEFFERSON STREETS IN THE SUBURB OF GRETNA.
1 ST
2 ND
3RD
4TH
ST.
ST.
ST.
ST.
NEWTON
JEFFERSON
DERBIGNY ST.

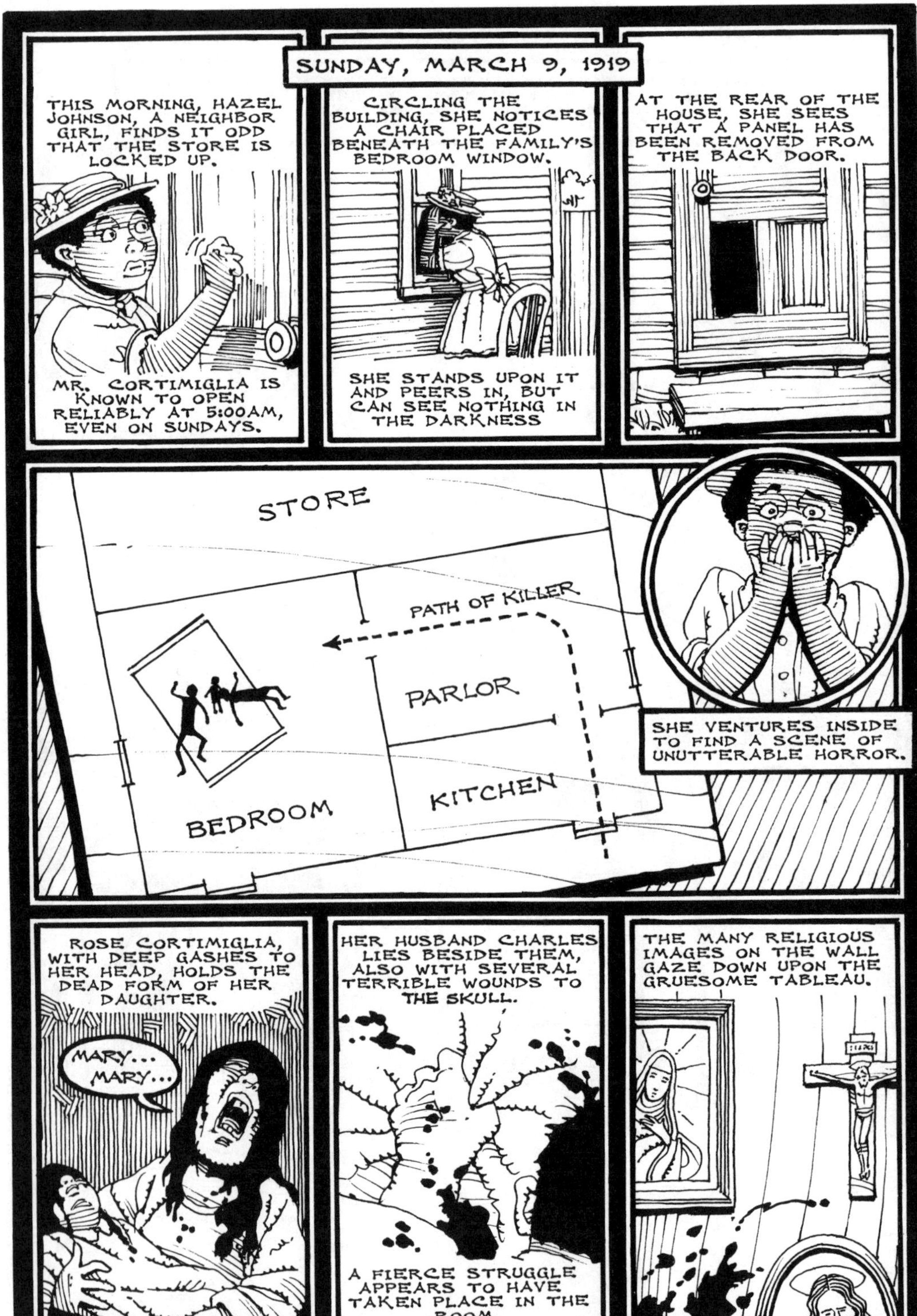
SUNDAY, MARCH 9, 1919
THIS MORNING, HAZEL JOHNSON, A NEIGHBOR GIRL, FINDS IT ODD THAT THE STORE IS LOCKED UP.
MR. CORTIMIGLIA IS KNOWN TO OPEN RELIABLY AT 5:00AM, EVEN ON SUNDAYS.
CIRCLING THE BUILDING, SHE NOTICES A CHAIR PLACED BENEATH THE FAMILY'S BEDROOM WINDOW.
SHE STANDS UPON IT AND PEERS IN, BUT CAN SEE NOTHING IN THE DARKNESS
AT THE REAR OF THE HOUSE, SHE SEES THAT A PANEL HAS BEEN REMOVED FROM THE BACK DOOR.
STORE
PATH OF KILLER
PARLOR
BEDROOM
KITCHEN
SHE VENTURES INSIDE TO FIND A SCENE OF UNUTTERABLE HORROR.
ROSE CORTIMIGLIA, WITH DEEP GASHES TO HER HEAD, HOLDS THE DEAD FORM OF HER DAUGHTER.
MARY... MARY...
HER HUSBAND CHARLES LIES BESIDE THEM, ALSO WITH SEVERAL TERRIBLE WOUNDS TO THE SKULL.
A FIERCE STRUGGLE APPEARS TO HAVE TAKEN PLACE IN THE ROOM.
THE MANY RELIGIOUS IMAGES ON THE WALL GAZE DOWN UPON THE GRUESOME TABLEAU.

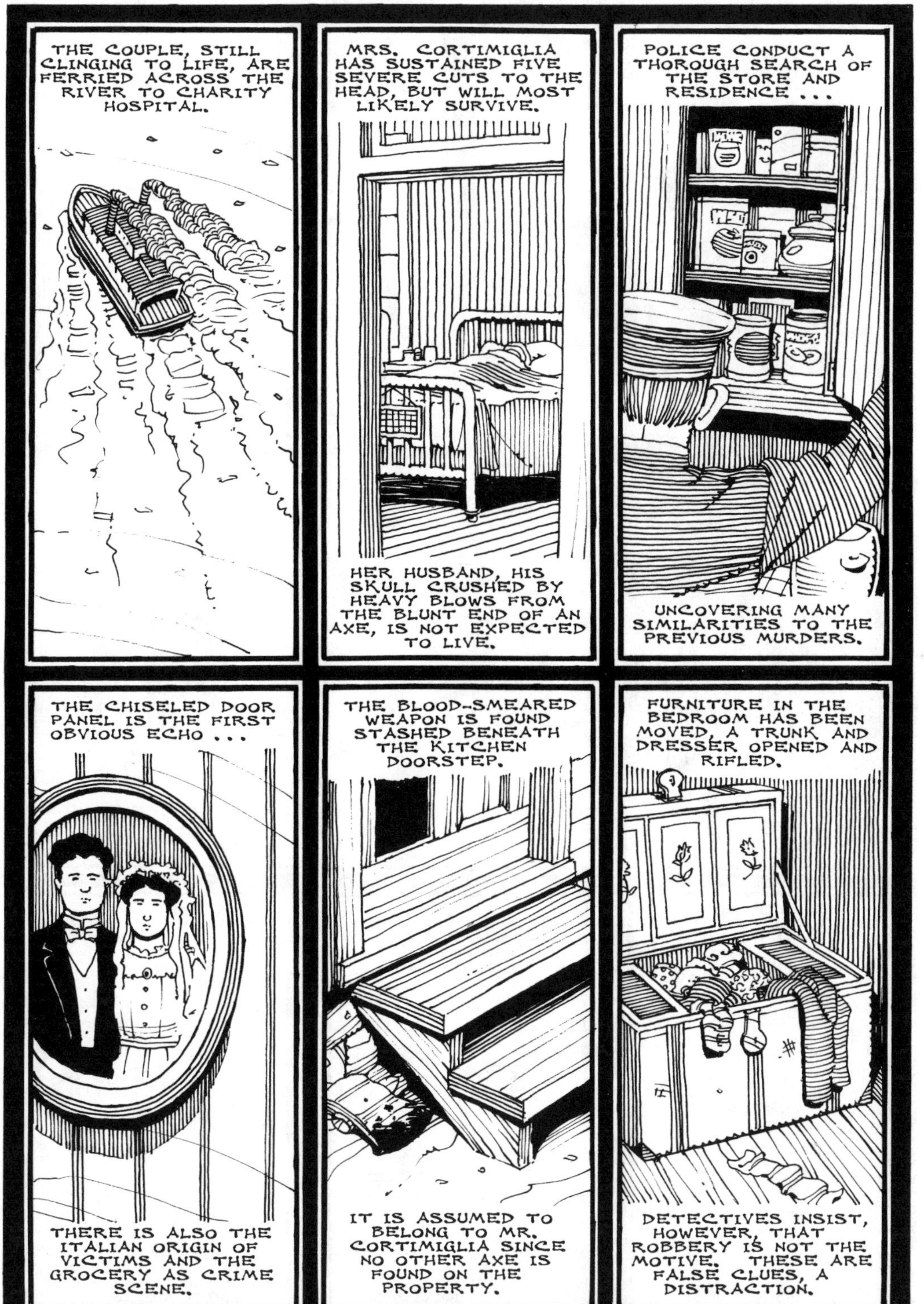
THE COUPLE, STILL CLINGING TO LIFE, ARE FERRIED ACROSS THE RIVER TO CHARITY HOSPITAL.
MRS. CORTIMIGLIA HAS SUSTAINED FIVE SEVERE CUTS TO THE HEAD, BUT WILL MOST LIKELY SURVIVE.
HER HUSBAND, HIS SKULL CRUSHED BY HEAVY BLOWS FROM THE BLUNT END OF AN AXE, IS NOT EXPECTED TO LIVE.
POLICE CONDUCT A THOROUGH SEARCH OF THE STORE AND RESIDENCE . . .
UNCOVERING MANY SIMILARITIES TO THE PREVIOUS MURDERS.
THE CHISELED DOOR PANEL IS THE FIRST OBVIOUS ECHO . . .
THERE IS ALSO THE ITALIAN ORIGIN OF VICTIMS AND THE GROCERY AS CRIME SCENE.
THE BLOOD-SMEARED WEAPON IS FOUND STASHED BENEATH THE KITCHEN DOORSTEP.
IT IS ASSUMED TO BELONG TO MR. CORTIMIGLIA SINCE NO OTHER AXE IS FOUND ON THE PROPERTY.
FURNITURE IN THE BEDROOM HAS BEEN MOVED, A TRUNK AND DRESSER OPENED AND RIFLED.
DETECTIVES INSIST, HOWEVER, THAT ROBBERY IS NOT THE MOTIVE. THESE ARE FALSE CLUES, A DISTRACTION.

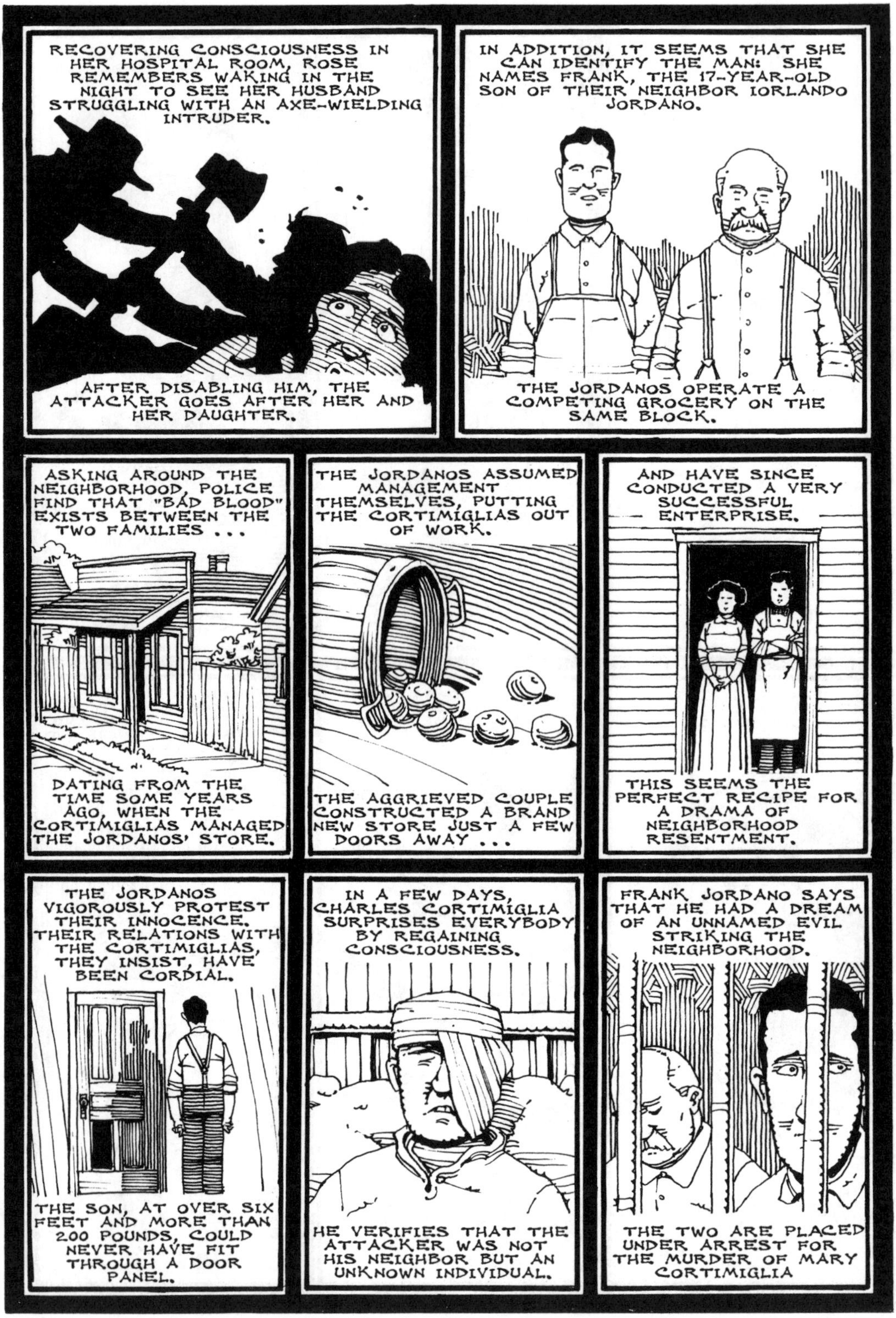
RECOVERING CONSCIOUSNESS IN HER HOSPITAL ROOM, ROSE REMEMBERS WAKING IN THE NIGHT TO SEE HER HUSBAND STRUGGLING WITH AN AXE-WIELDING INTRUDER.
AFTER DISABLING HIM, THE ATTACKER GOES AFTER HER AND HER DAUGHTER.
IN ADDITION, IT SEEMS THAT SHE CAN IDENTIFY THE MAN: SHE NAMES FRANK, THE 17-YEAR-OLD SON OF THEIR NEIGHBOR IORLANDO JORDANO.
THE JORDANOS OPERATE A COMPETING GROCERY ON THE SAME BLOCK.
ASKING AROUND THE NEIGHBORHOOD, POLICE FIND THAT "BAD BLOOD" EXISTS BETWEEN THE TWO FAMILIES ...
DATING FROM THE TIME SOME YEARS AGO, WHEN THE CORTIMIGLIAS MANAGED THE JORDANOS' STORE.
THE JORDANOS ASSUMED MANAGEMENT THEMSELVES, PUTTING THE CORTIMIGLIAS OUT OF WORK.
THE AGGRIEVED COUPLE CONSTRUCTED A BRAND NEW STORE JUST A FEW DOORS AWAY ...
AND HAVE SINCE CONDUCTED A VERY SUCCESSFUL ENTERPRISE.
THIS SEEMS THE PERFECT RECIPE FOR A DRAMA OF NEIGHBORHOOD RESENTMENT.
THE JORDANOS VIGOROUSLY PROTEST THEIR INNOCENCE. THEIR RELATIONS WITH THE CORTIMIGLIAS, THEY INSIST, HAVE BEEN CORDIAL.
THE SON, AT OVER SIX FEET AND MORE THAN 200 POUNDS, COULD NEVER HAVE FIT THROUGH A DOOR PANEL.
IN A FEW DAYS, CHARLES CORTIMIGLIA SURPRISES EVERYBODY BY REGAINING CONSCIOUSNESS.
HE VERIFIES THAT THE ATTACKER WAS NOT HIS NEIGHBOR BUT AN UNKNOWN INDIVIDUAL.
FRANK JORDANO SAYS THAT HE HAD A DREAM OF AN UNNAMED EVIL STRIKING THE NEIGHBORHOOD.
THE TWO ARE PLACED UNDER ARREST FOR THE MURDER OF MARY CORTIMIGLIA

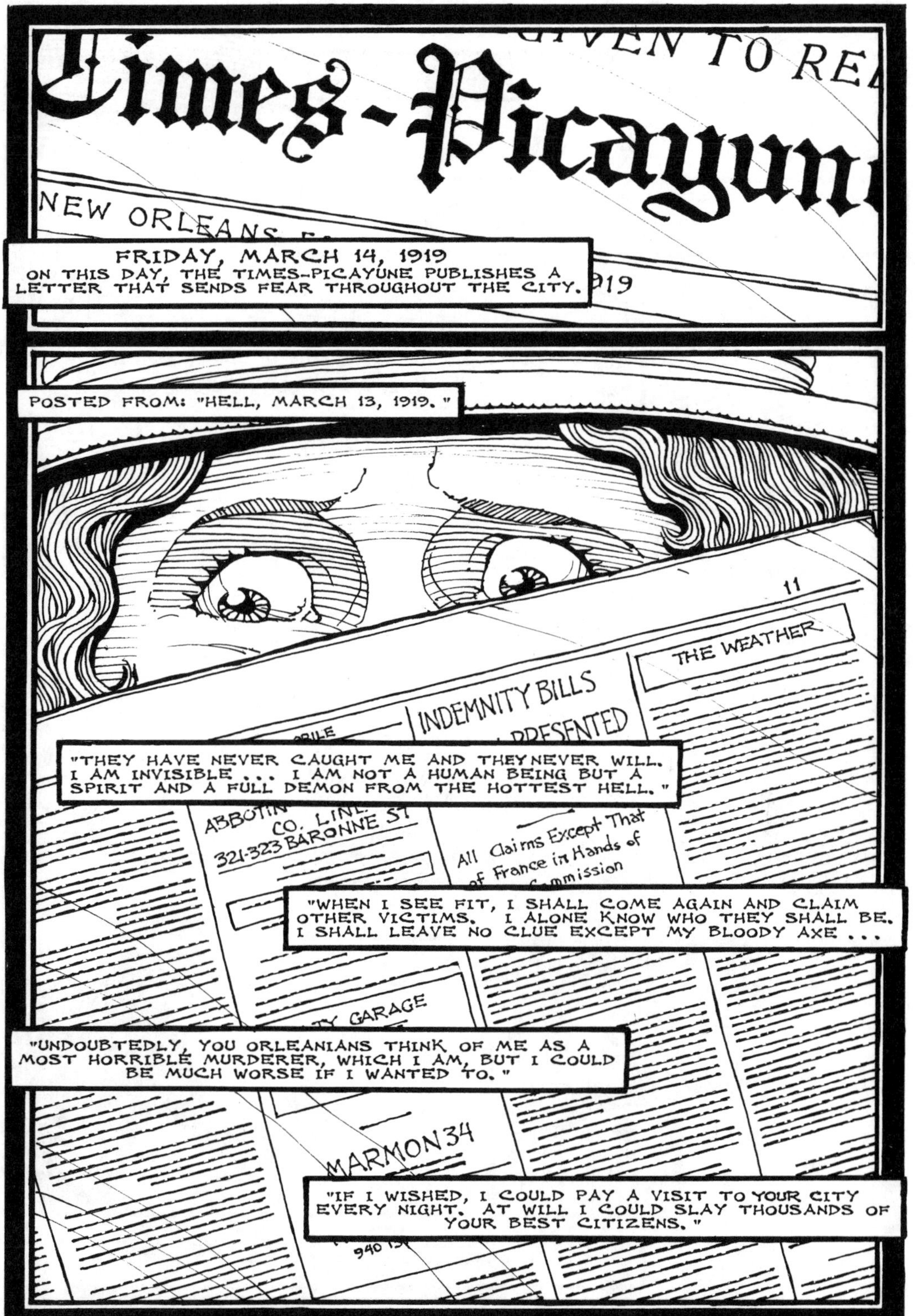
Times-Picayune
NEW ORLEANS
FRIDAY, MARCH 14, 1919
ON THIS DAY, THE TIMES-PICAYUNE PUBLISHES A LETTER THAT SENDS FEAR THROUGHOUT THE CITY.
POSTED FROM: "HELL, MARCH 13, 1919."
11
THE WEATHER
INDEMNITY BILLS
PRESENTED
"THEY HAVE NEVER CAUGHT ME AND THEY NEVER WILL. I AM INVISIBLE . . . I AM NOT A HUMAN BEING BUT A SPIRIT AND A FULL DEMON FROM THE HOTTEST HELL."
CO. LINE
321-323 BARONNE ST
All Claims Except That of France in Hands of
"WHEN I SEE FIT, I SHALL COME AGAIN AND CLAIM OTHER VICTIMS. I ALONE KNOW WHO THEY SHALL BE. I SHALL LEAVE NO CLUE EXCEPT MY BLOODY AXE . . .
GARAGE
"UNDOUBTEDLY, YOU ORLEANIANS THINK OF ME AS A MOST HORRIBLE MURDERER, WHICH I AM, BUT I COULD BE MUCH WORSE IF I WANTED TO."
MARMON 34
"IF I WISHED, I COULD PAY A VISIT TO YOUR CITY EVERY NIGHT. AT WILL I COULD SLAY THOUSANDS OF YOUR BEST CITIZENS."

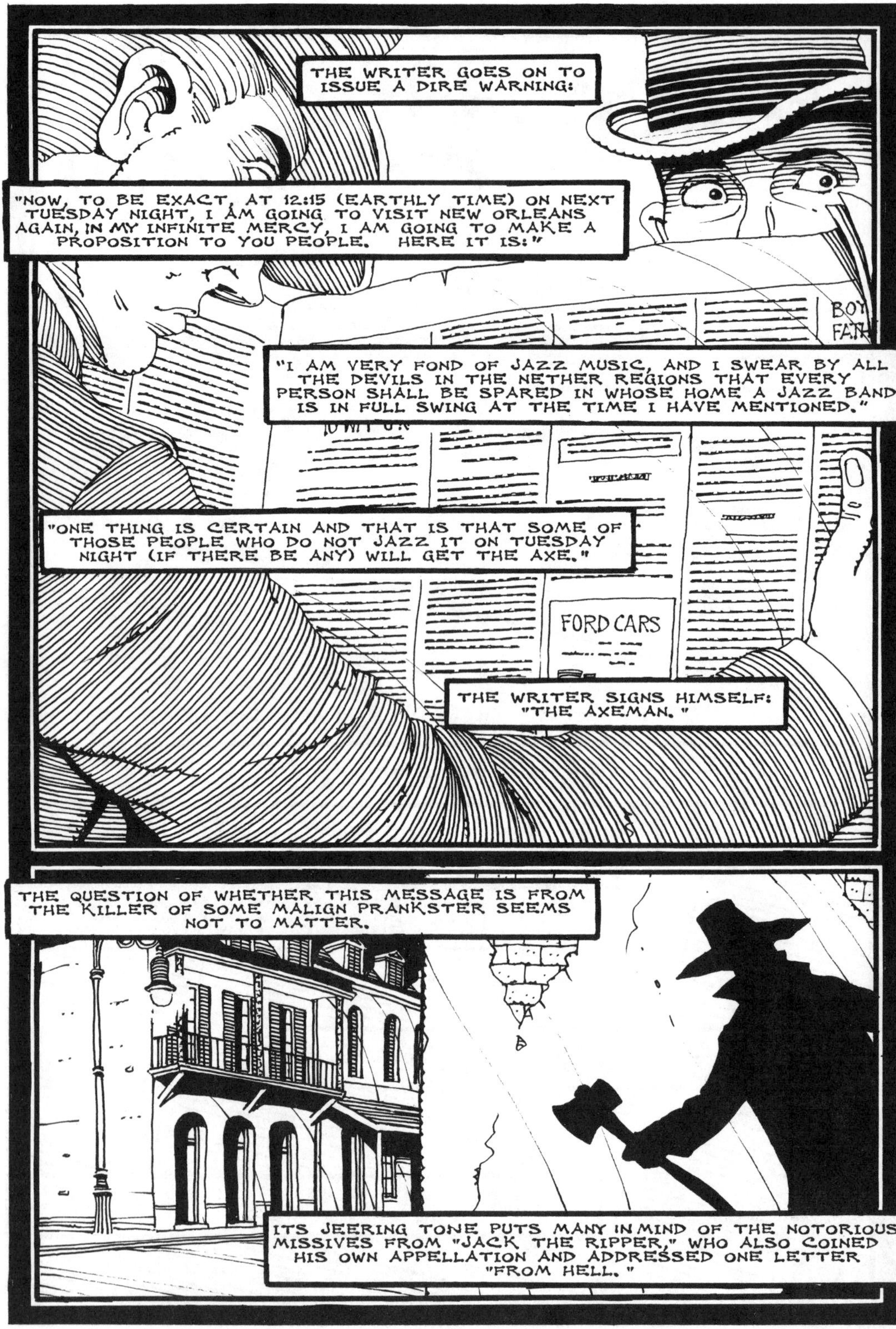
THE WRITER GOES ON TO ISSUE A DIRE WARNING:
"NOW, TO BE EXACT, AT 12:15 (EARTHLY TIME) ON NEXT TUESDAY NIGHT, I AM GOING TO VISIT NEW ORLEANS AGAIN, IN MY INFINITE MERCY, I AM GOING TO MAKE A PROPOSITION TO YOU PEOPLE. HERE IT IS:"
"I AM VERY FOND OF JAZZ MUSIC, AND I SWEAR BY ALL THE DEVILS IN THE NETHER REGIONS THAT EVERY PERSON SHALL BE SPARED IN WHOSE HOME A JAZZ BAND IS IN FULL SWING AT THE TIME I HAVE MENTIONED."
"ONE THING IS CERTAIN AND THAT IS THAT SOME OF THOSE PEOPLE WHO DO NOT JAZZ IT ON TUESDAY NIGHT (IF THERE BE ANY) WILL GET THE AXE."
FORD CARS
THE WRITER SIGNS HIMSELF: "THE AXEMAN."
THE QUESTION OF WHETHER THIS MESSAGE IS FROM THE KILLER OF SOME MALIGN PRANKSTER SEEMS NOT TO MATTER.
ITS JEERING TONE PUTS MANY IN MIND OF THE NOTORIOUS MISSIVES FROM "JACK THE RIPPER," WHO ALSO COINED HIS OWN APPELLATION AND ADDRESSED ONE LETTER "FROM HELL."

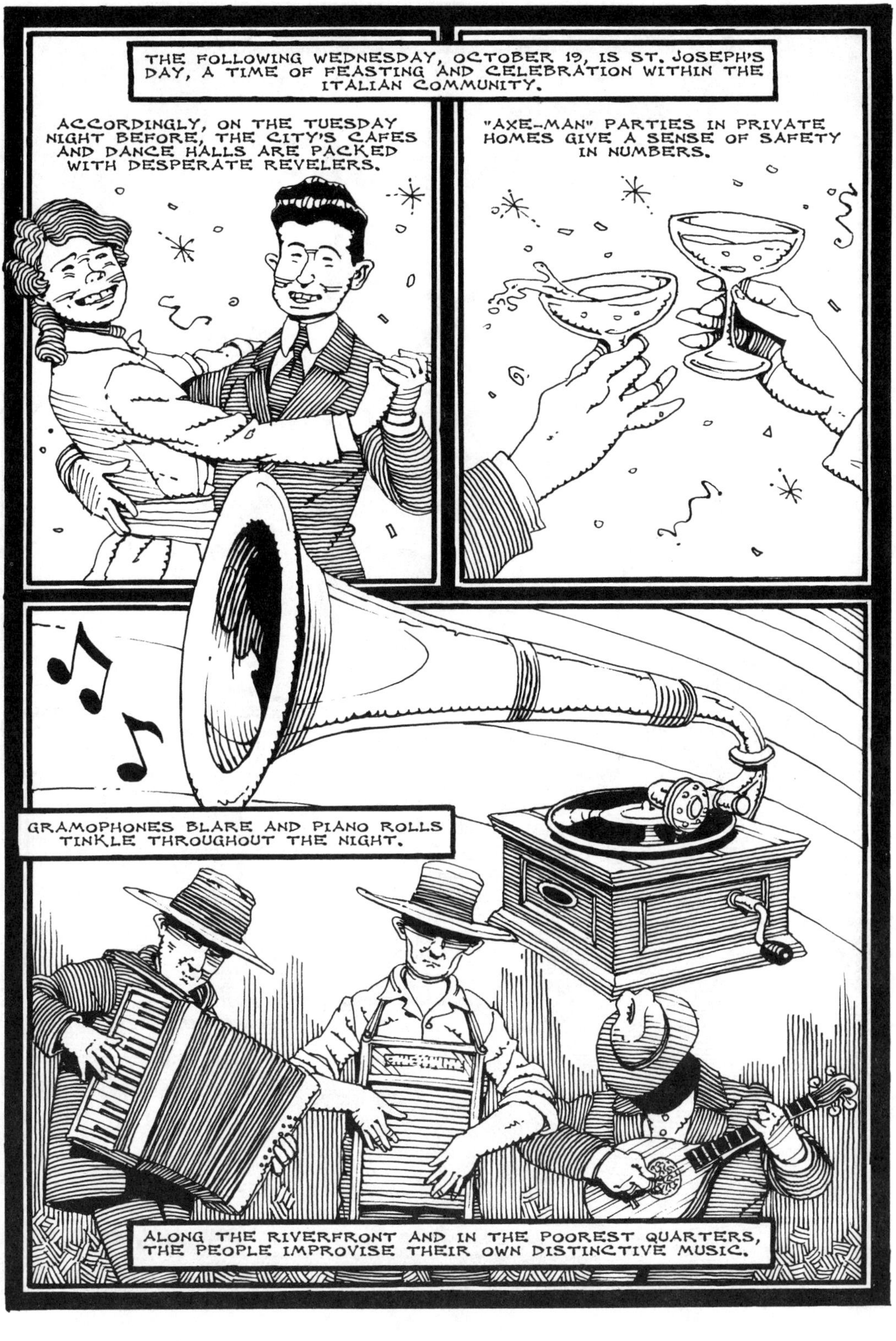
THE FOLLOWING WEDNESDAY, OCTOBER 19, IS ST. JOSEPH'S DAY, A TIME OF FEASTING AND CELEBRATION WITHIN THE ITALIAN COMMUNITY.
ACCORDINGLY, ON THE TUESDAY NIGHT BEFORE, THE CITY'S CAFES AND DANCE HALLS ARE PACKED WITH DESPERATE REVELERS.
"AXE-MAN" PARTIES IN PRIVATE HOMES GIVE A SENSE OF SAFETY IN NUMBERS.
GRAMOPHONES BLARE AND PIANO ROLLS TINKLE THROUGHOUT THE NIGHT.
ALONG THE RIVERFRONT AND IN THE POOREST QUARTERS, THE PEOPLE IMPROVISE THEIR OWN DISTINCTIVE MUSIC.

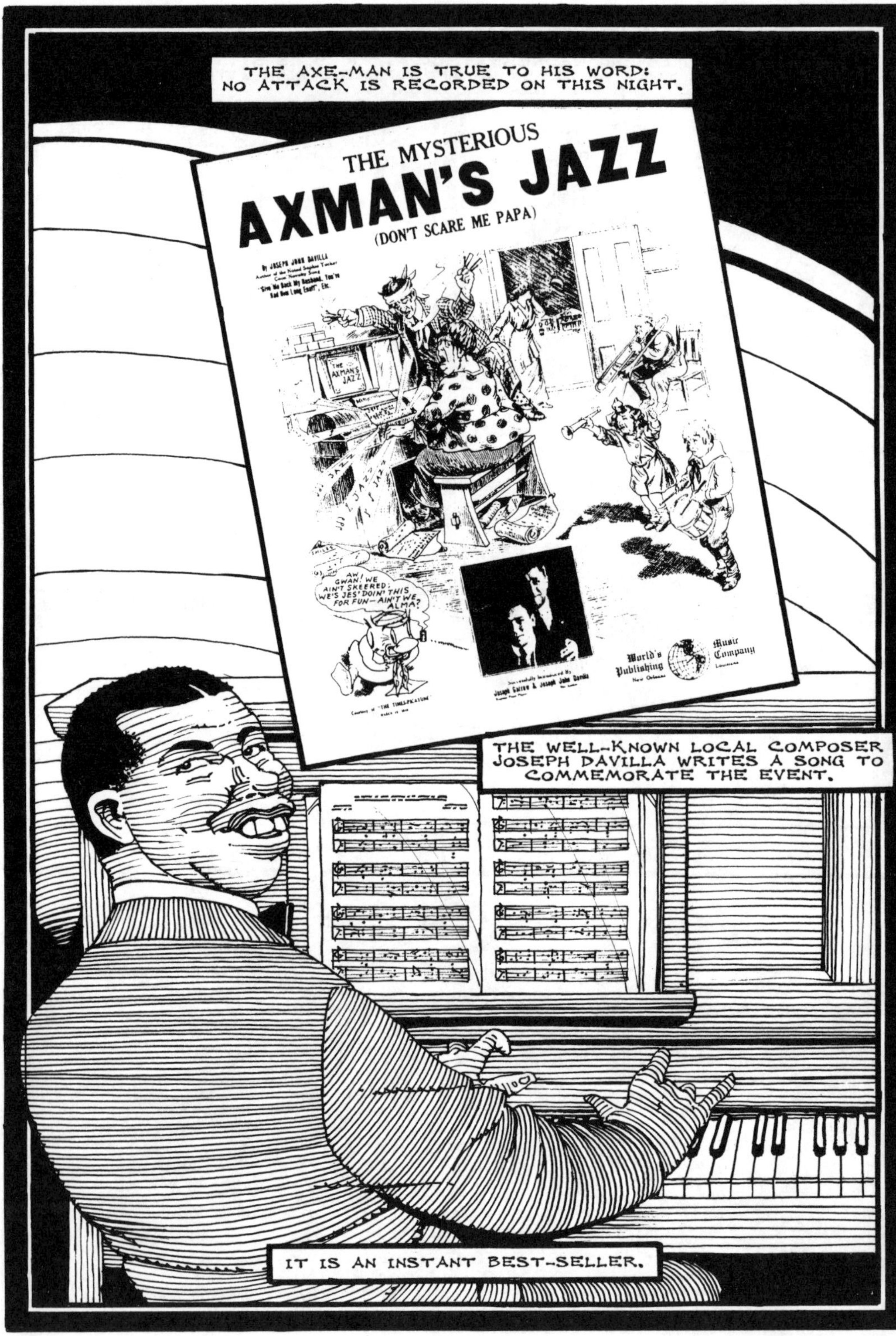
THE AXE-MAN IS TRUE TO HIS WORD: NO ATTACK IS RECORDED ON THIS NIGHT.
THE MYSTERIOUS
AXMAN'S JAZZ
(DON'T SCARE ME PAPA)
By JOSEPH JOHN DAVILLA
THE AXMAN'S JAZZ
AW! GWAN! WE AIN'T SKEERED; WE'S JES' DOIN' THIS FOR FUN—AIN'T WE, ALMA?
World's Publishing Music Company
THE WELL-KNOWN LOCAL COMPOSER JOSEPH DAVILLA WRITES A SONG TO COMMEMORATE THE EVENT.
IT IS AN INSTANT BEST-SELLER.

PART V

THE FINAL OUTRAGE

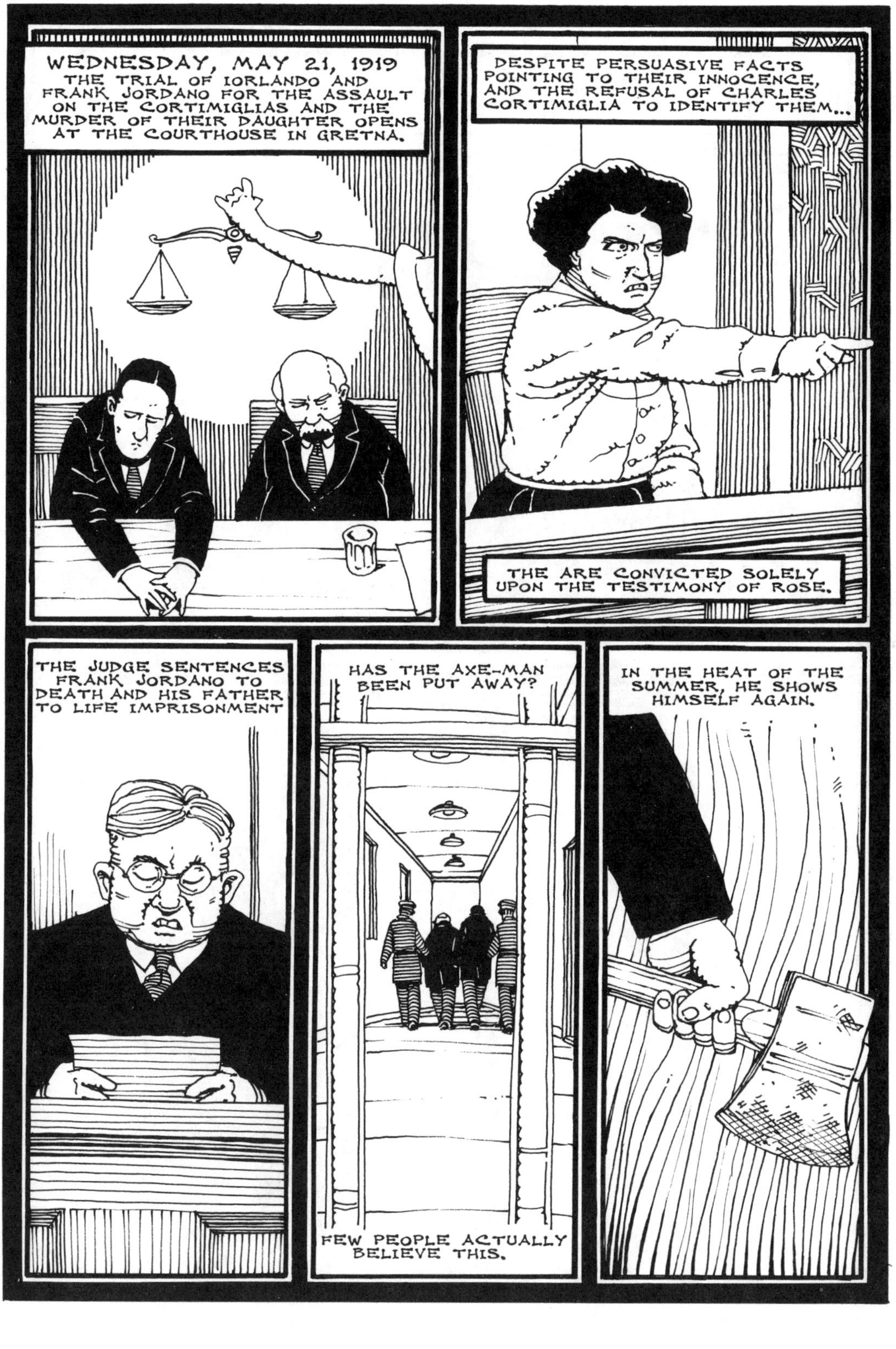
WEDNESDAY, MAY 21, 1919
THE TRIAL OF IORLANDO AND FRANK JORDANO FOR THE ASSAULT ON THE CORTIMIGLIAS AND THE MURDER OF THEIR DAUGHTER OPENS AT THE COURTHOUSE IN GRETNA.
DESPITE PERSUASIVE FACTS POINTING TO THEIR INNOCENCE, AND THE REFUSAL OF CHARLES CORTIMIGLIA TO IDENTIFY THEM...
THE ARE CONVICTED SOLELY UPON THE TESTIMONY OF ROSE.
THE JUDGE SENTENCES FRANK JORDANO TO DEATH AND HIS FATHER TO LIFE IMPRISONMENT
HAS THE AXE-MAN BEEN PUT AWAY?
FEW PEOPLE ACTUALLY BELIEVE THIS.
IN THE HEAT OF THE SUMMER, HE SHOWS HIMSELF AGAIN.

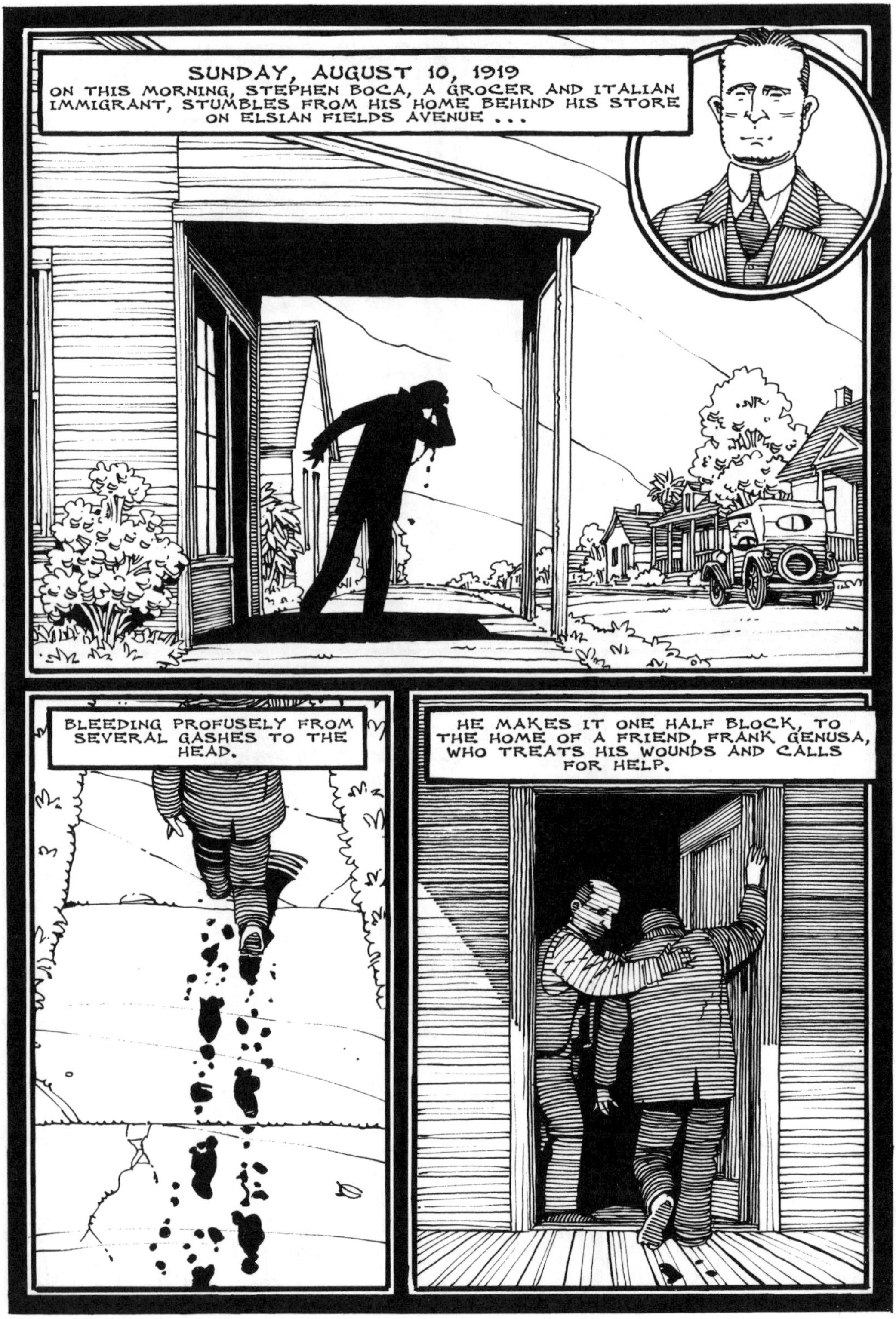
SUNDAY, AUGUST 10, 1919
ON THIS MORNING, STEPHEN BOCA, A GROCER AND ITALIAN IMMIGRANT, STUMBLES FROM HIS HOME BEHIND HIS STORE ON ELSIAN FIELDS AVENUE ...
BLEEDING PROFUSELY FROM SEVERAL GASHES TO THE HEAD.
HE MAKES IT ONE HALF BLOCK, TO THE HOME OF A FRIEND, FRANK GENUSA, WHO TREATS HIS WOUNDS AND CALLS FOR HELP.

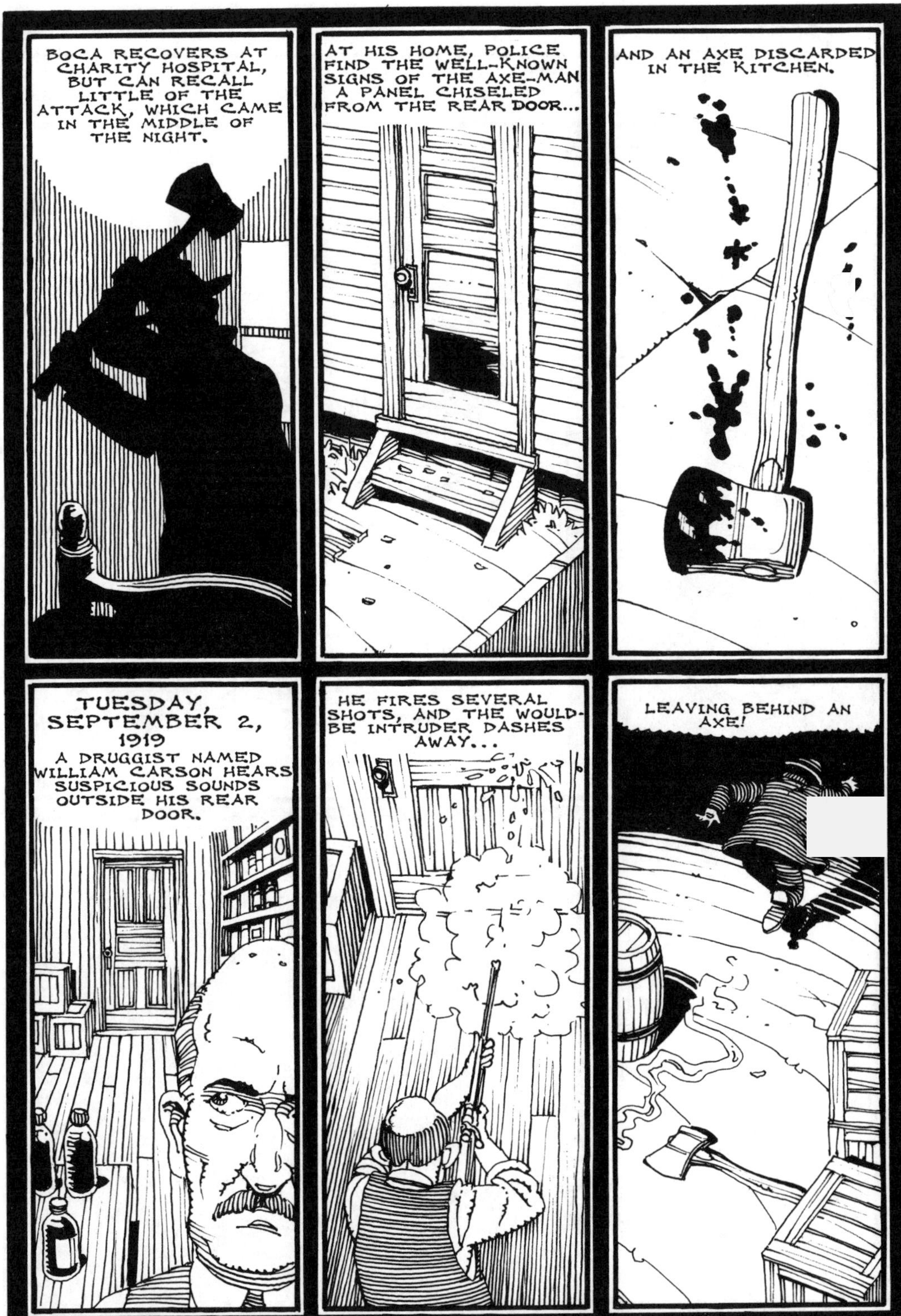
BOCA RECOVERS AT CHARITY HOSPITAL, BUT CAN RECALL LITTLE OF THE ATTACK, WHICH CAME IN THE MIDDLE OF THE NIGHT.
AT HIS HOME, POLICE FIND THE WELL-KNOWN SIGNS OF THE AXE-MAN A PANEL CHISELED FROM THE REAR DOOR...
AND AN AXE DISCARDED IN THE KITCHEN.
TUESDAY, SEPTEMBER 2, 1919
A DRUGGIST NAMED WILLIAM CARSON HEARS SUSPICIOUS SOUNDS OUTSIDE HIS REAR DOOR.
HE FIRES SEVERAL SHOTS, AND THE WOULD-BE INTRUDER DASHES AWAY...
LEAVING BEHIND AN AXE!

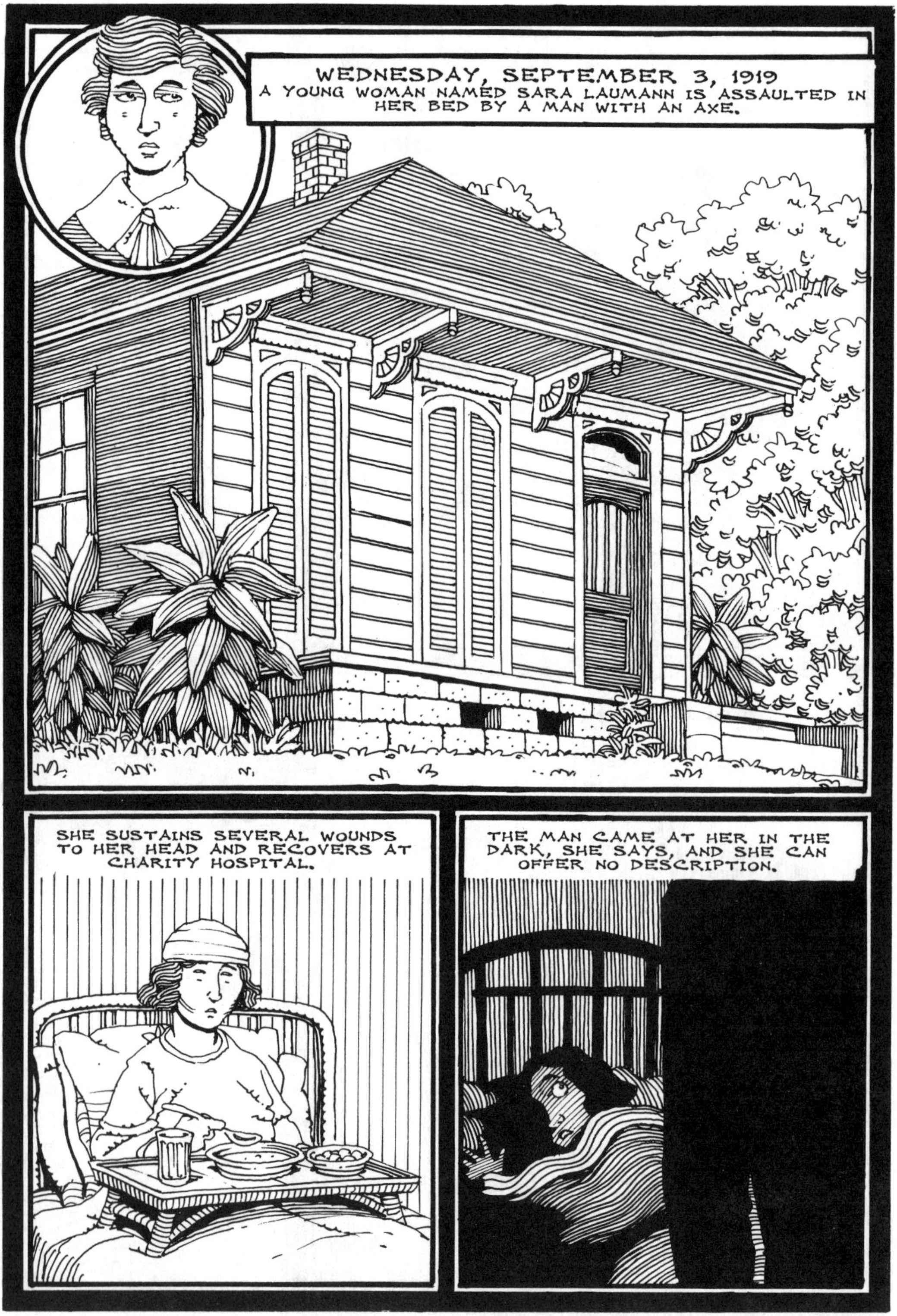
WEDNESDAY, SEPTEMBER 3, 1919
A YOUNG WOMAN NAMED SARA LAUMANN IS ASSAULTED IN HER BED BY A MAN WITH AN AXE.
SHE SUSTAINS SEVERAL WOUNDS TO HER HEAD AND RECOVERS AT CHARITY HOSPITAL.
THE MAN CAME AT HER IN THE DARK, SHE SAYS, AND SHE CAN OFFER NO DESCRIPTION.

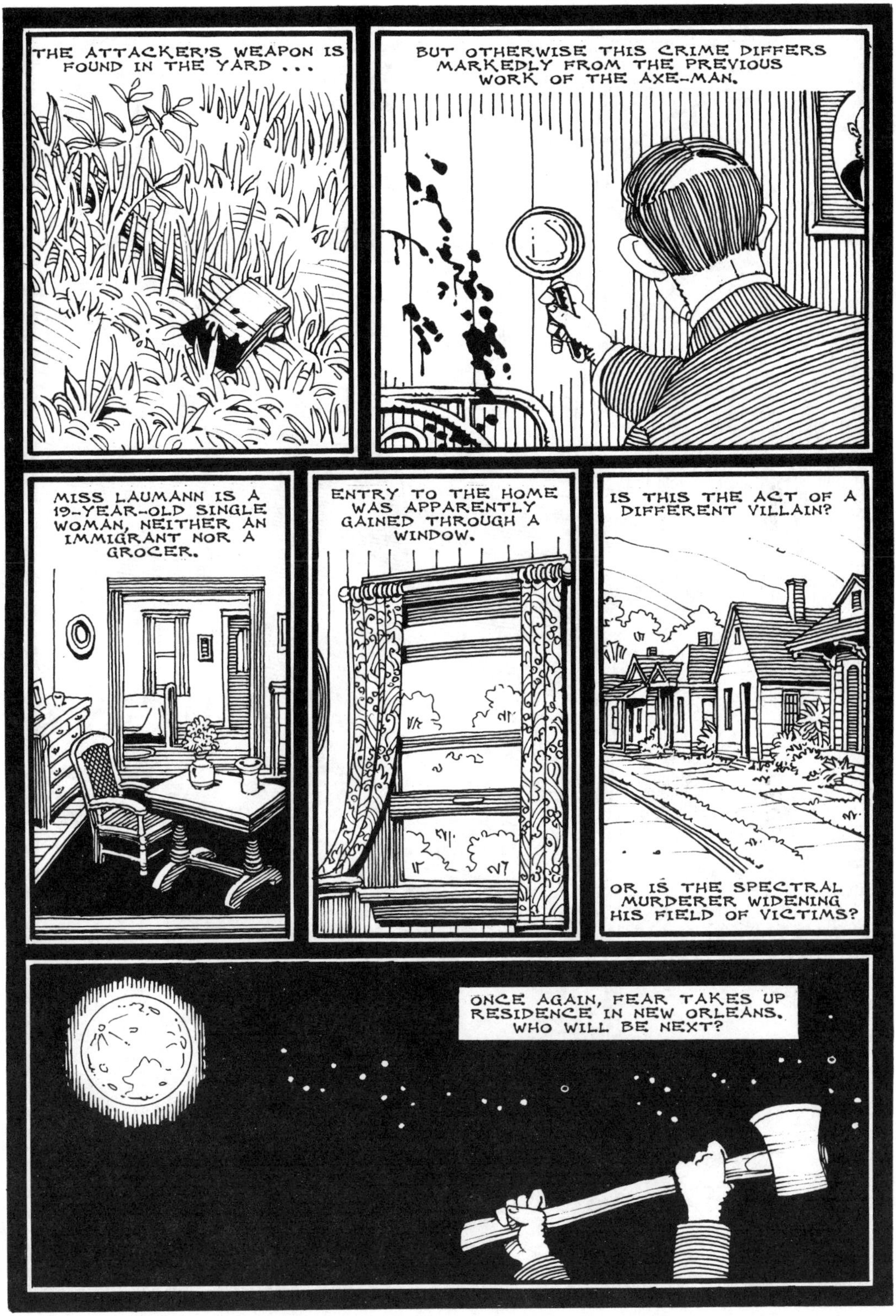
THE ATTACKER'S WEAPON IS FOUND IN THE YARD ...
BUT OTHERWISE THIS CRIME DIFFERS MARKEDLY FROM THE PREVIOUS WORK OF THE AXE-MAN.
MISS LAUMANN IS A 19-YEAR-OLD SINGLE WOMAN, NEITHER AN IMMIGRANT NOR A GROCER.
ENTRY TO THE HOME WAS APPARENTLY GAINED THROUGH A WINDOW.
IS THIS THE ACT OF A DIFFERENT VILLAIN?
OR IS THE SPECTRAL MURDERER WIDENING HIS FIELD OF VICTIMS?
ONCE AGAIN, FEAR TAKES UP RESIDENCE IN NEW ORLEANS. WHO WILL BE NEXT?

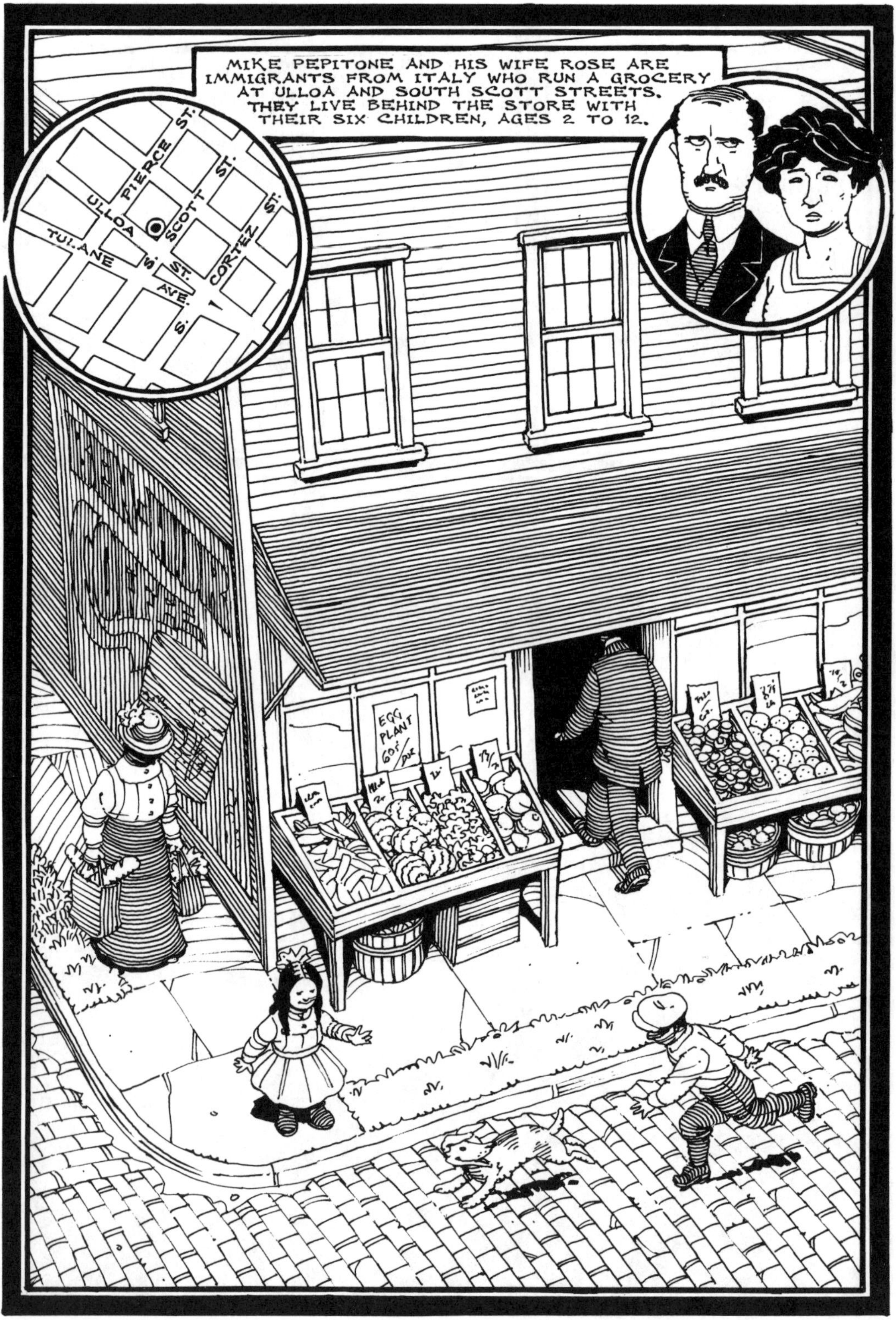
MIKE PEPITONE AND HIS WIFE ROSE ARE IMMIGRANTS FROM ITALY WHO RUN A GROCERY AT ULLOA AND SOUTH SCOTT STREETS. THEY LIVE BEHIND THE STORE WITH THEIR SIX CHILDREN, AGES 2 TO 12.
PIERCE ST.
ULLOA
S. SCOTT ST.
CORTEZ ST.
TULANE AVE.
S.
EGG PLANT
60¢ DOZ

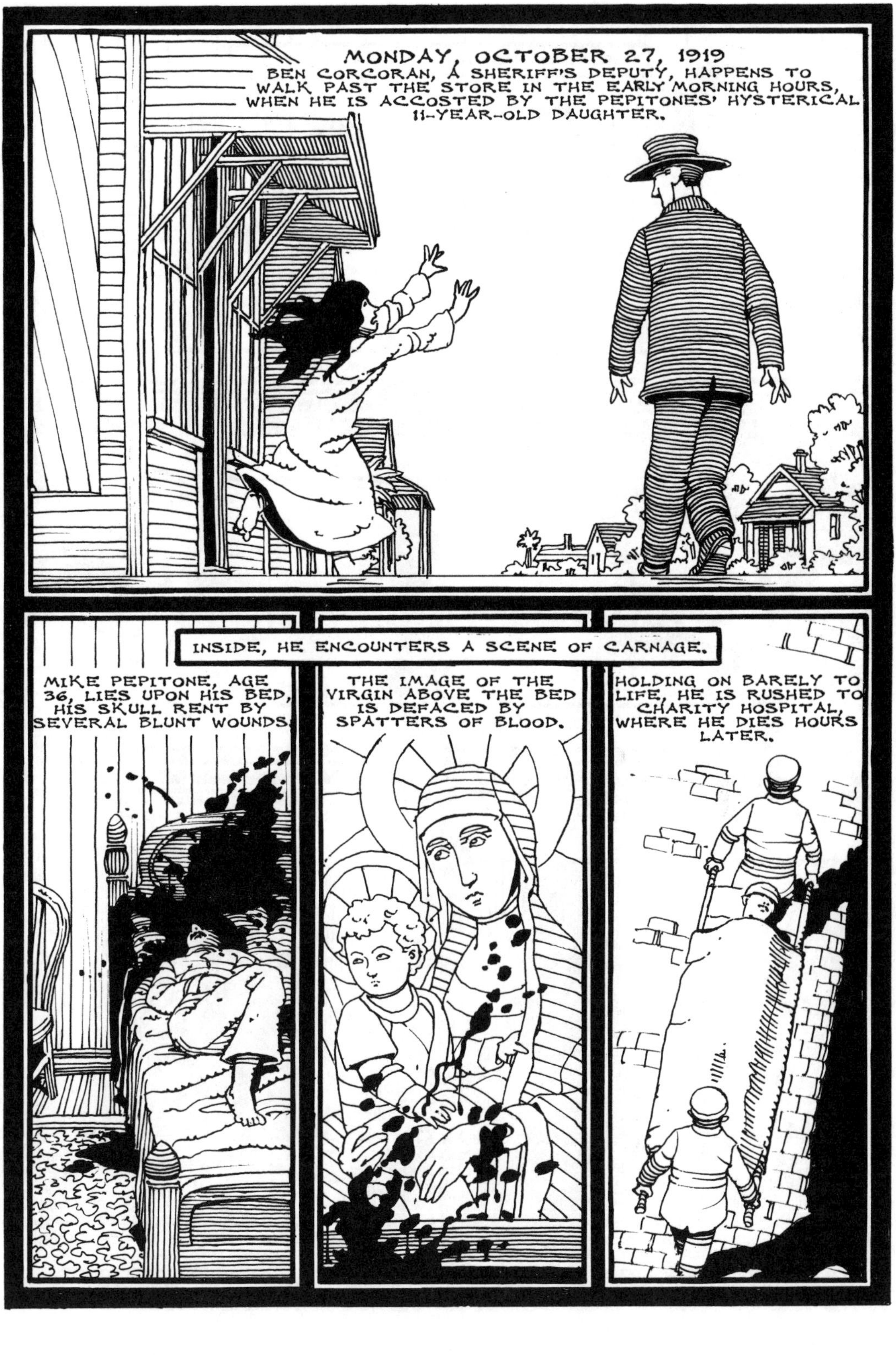
MONDAY, OCTOBER 27, 1919
BEN CORCORAN, A SHERIFF'S DEPUTY, HAPPENS TO WALK PAST THE STORE IN THE EARLY MORNING HOURS, WHEN HE IS ACCOSTED BY THE PEPITONES' HYSTERICAL 11-YEAR-OLD DAUGHTER.
INSIDE, HE ENCOUNTERS A SCENE OF CARNAGE.
MIKE PEPITONE, AGE 36, LIES UPON HIS BED, HIS SKULL RENT BY SEVERAL BLUNT WOUNDS.
THE IMAGE OF THE VIRGIN ABOVE THE BED IS DEFACED BY SPATTERS OF BLOOD.
HOLDING ON BARELY TO LIFE, HE IS RUSHED TO CHARITY HOSPITAL, WHERE HE DIES HOURS LATER.

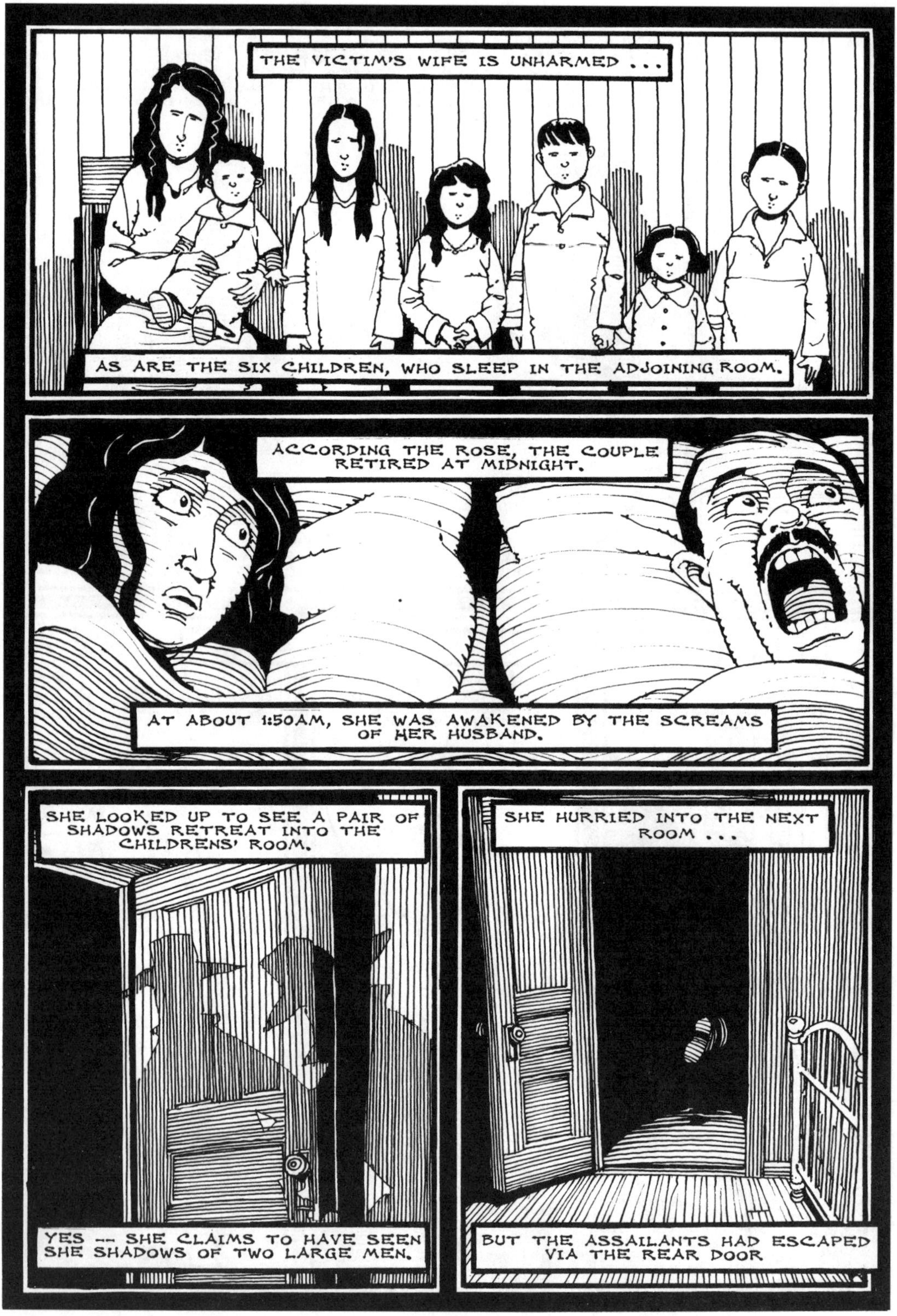
THE VICTIM'S WIFE IS UNHARMED ...
AS ARE THE SIX CHILDREN, WHO SLEEP IN THE ADJOINING ROOM.
ACCORDING THE ROSE, THE COUPLE RETIRED AT MIDNIGHT.
AT ABOUT 1:50AM, SHE WAS AWAKENED BY THE SCREAMS OF HER HUSBAND.
SHE LOOKED UP TO SEE A PAIR OF SHADOWS RETREAT INTO THE CHILDRENS' ROOM.
YES -- SHE CLAIMS TO HAVE SEEN SHE SHADOWS OF TWO LARGE MEN.
SHE HURRIED INTO THE NEXT ROOM ...
BUT THE ASSAILANTS HAD ESCAPED VIA THE REAR DOOR

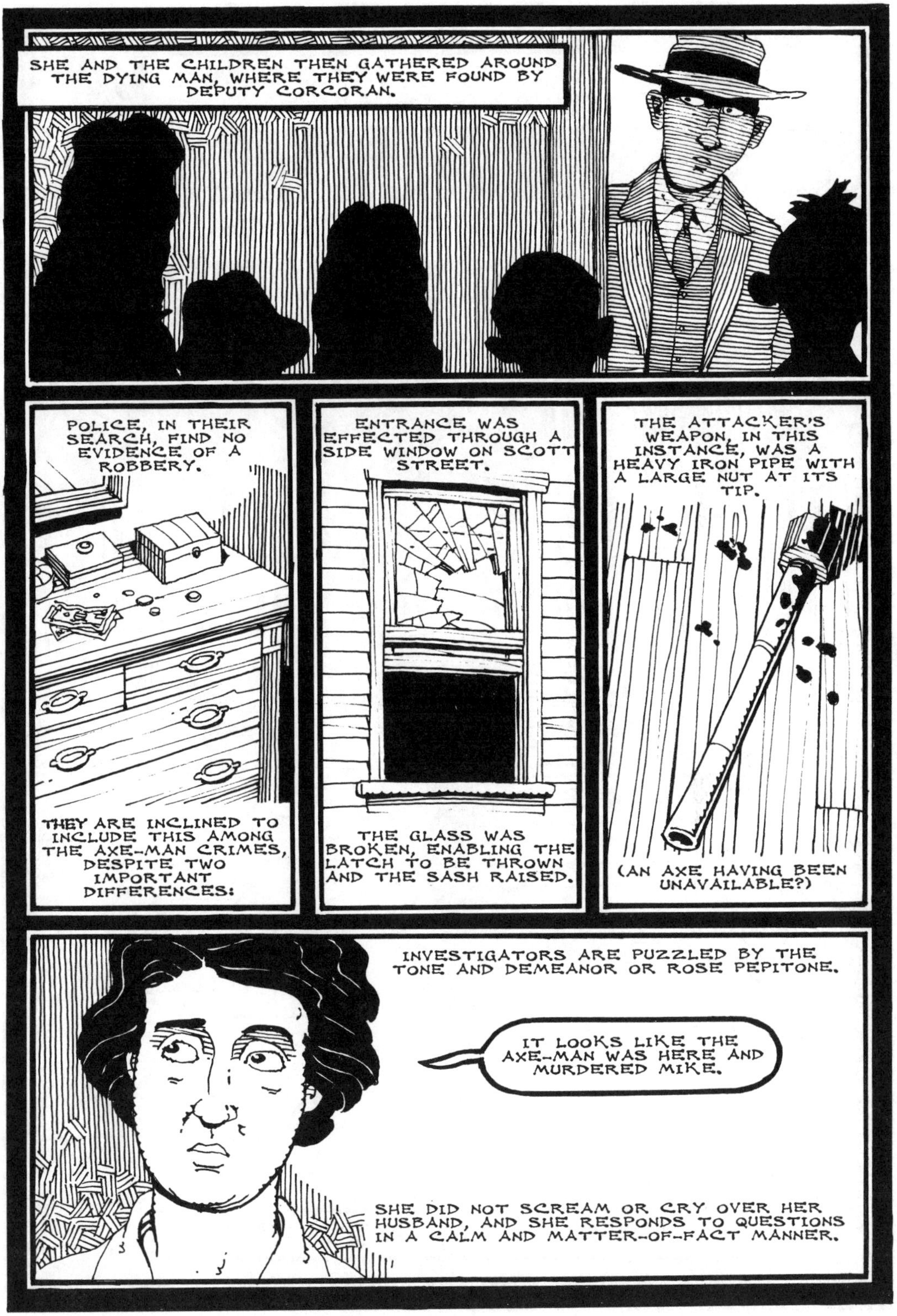
SHE AND THE CHILDREN THEN GATHERED AROUND THE DYING MAN, WHERE THEY WERE FOUND BY DEPUTY CORCORAN.
POLICE, IN THEIR SEARCH, FIND NO EVIDENCE OF A ROBBERY.
THEY ARE INCLINED TO INCLUDE THIS AMONG THE AXE-MAN CRIMES, DESPITE TWO IMPORTANT DIFFERENCES:
ENTRANCE WAS EFFECTED THROUGH A SIDE WINDOW ON SCOTT STREET.
THE GLASS WAS BROKEN, ENABLING THE LATCH TO BE THROWN AND THE SASH RAISED.
THE ATTACKER'S WEAPON, IN THIS INSTANCE, WAS A HEAVY IRON PIPE WITH A LARGE NUT AT ITS TIP.
(AN AXE HAVING BEEN UNAVAILABLE?)
INVESTIGATORS ARE PUZZLED BY THE TONE AND DEMEANOR OR ROSE PEPITONE.
IT LOOKS LIKE THE AXE-MAN WAS HERE AND MURDERED MIKE.
SHE DID NOT SCREAM OR CRY OVER HER HUSBAND, AND SHE RESPONDS TO QUESTIONS IN A CALM AND MATTER-OF-FACT MANNER.

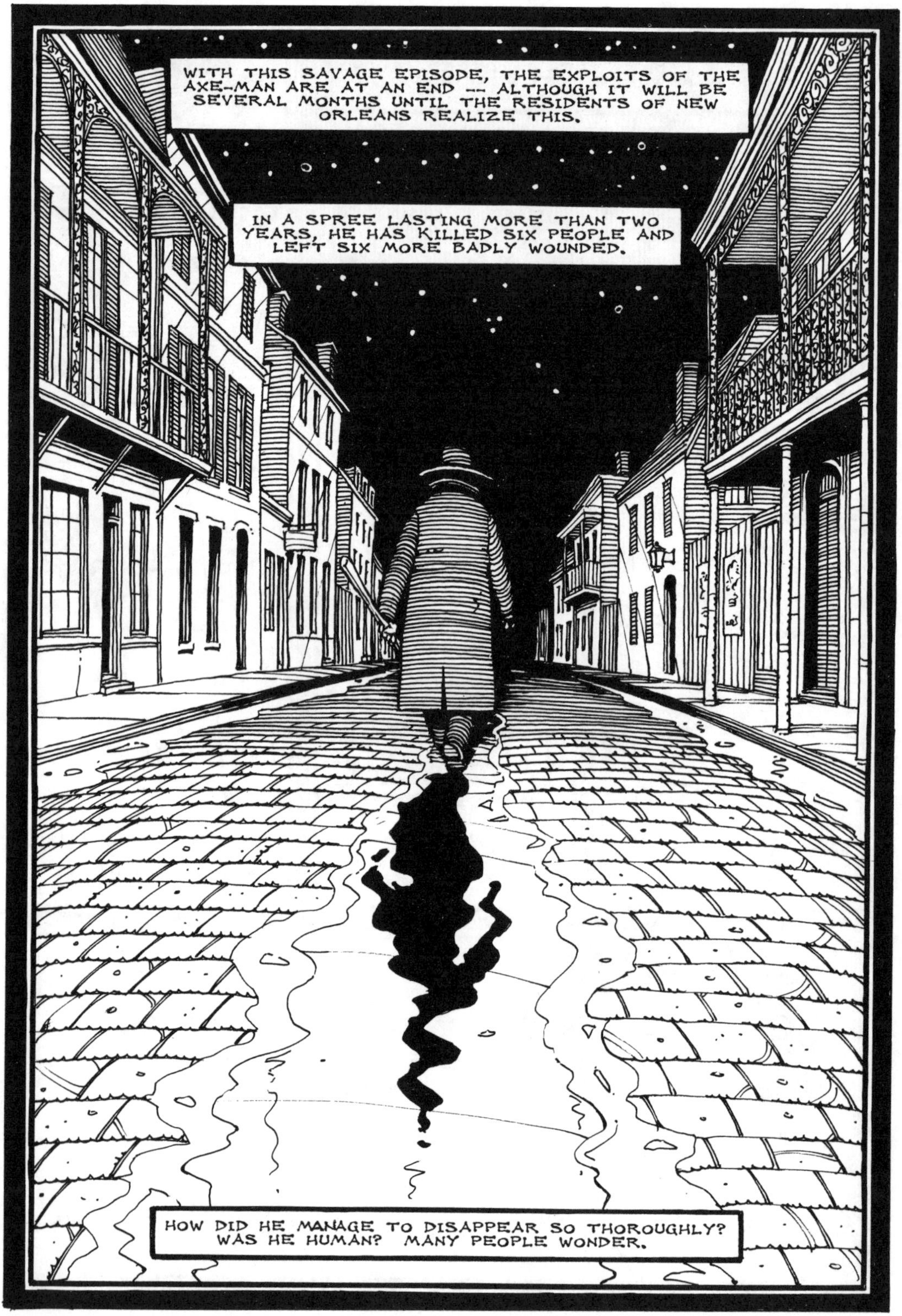
WITH THIS SAVAGE EPISODE, THE EXPLOITS OF THE AXE-MAN ARE AT AN END -- ALTHOUGH IT WILL BE SEVERAL MONTHS UNTIL THE RESIDENTS OF NEW ORLEANS REALIZE THIS.
IN A SPREE LASTING MORE THAN TWO YEARS, HE HAS KILLED SIX PEOPLE AND LEFT SIX MORE BADLY WOUNDED.
HOW DID HE MANAGE TO DISAPPEAR SO THOROUGHLY? WAS HE HUMAN? MANY PEOPLE WONDER.

PART VI

WHO WAS IT?

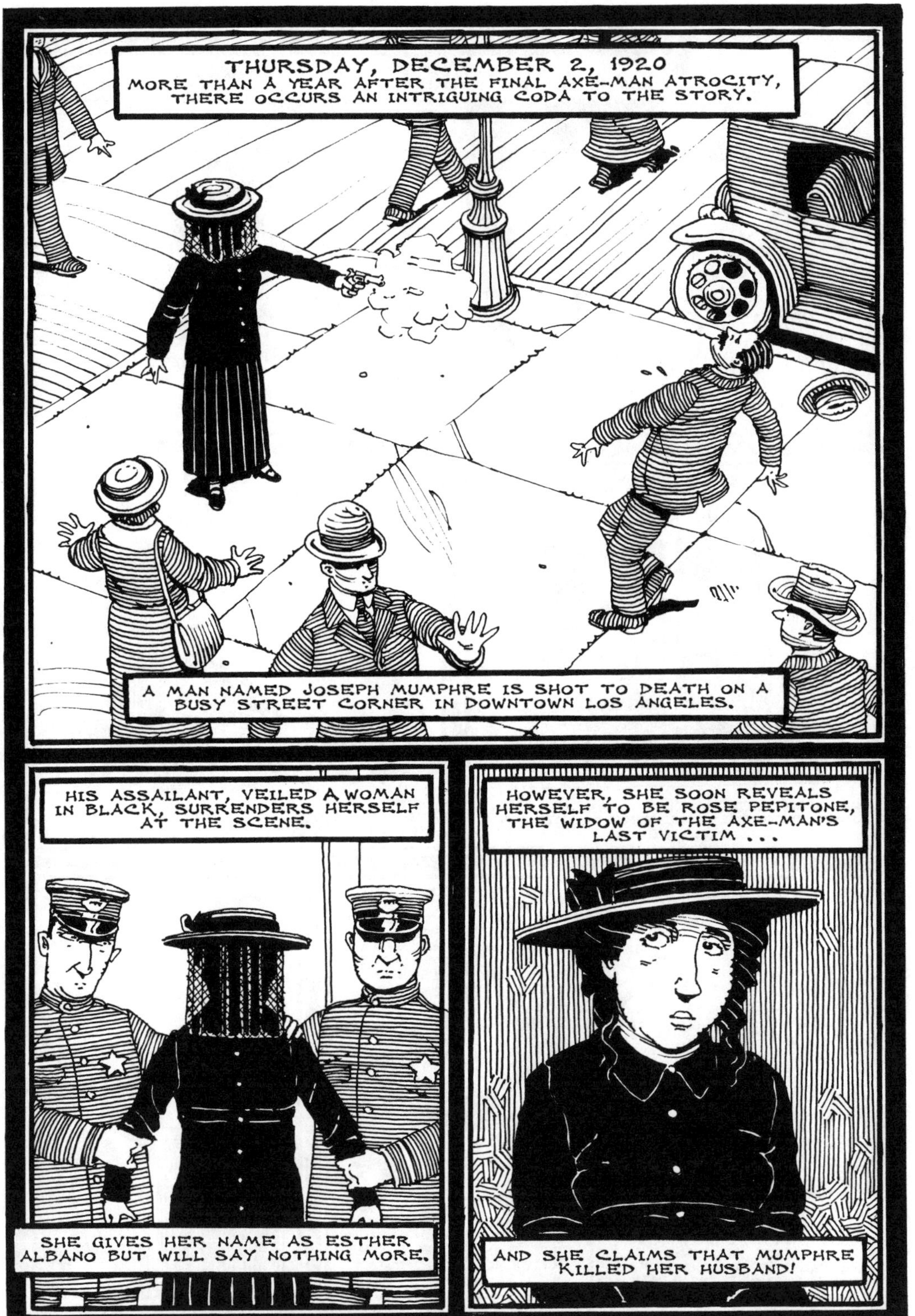
THURSDAY, DECEMBER 2, 1920
MORE THAN A YEAR AFTER THE FINAL AXE-MAN ATROCITY, THERE OCCURS AN INTRIGUING CODA TO THE STORY.
A MAN NAMED JOSEPH MUMPHRE IS SHOT TO DEATH ON A BUSY STREET CORNER IN DOWNTOWN LOS ANGELES.
HIS ASSAILANT, VEILED A WOMAN IN BLACK, SURRENDERS HERSELF AT THE SCENE.
SHE GIVES HER NAME AS ESTHER ALBANO BUT WILL SAY NOTHING MORE.
HOWEVER, SHE SOON REVEALS HERSELF TO BE ROSE PEPITONE, THE WIDOW OF THE AXE-MAN'S LAST VICTIM ...
AND SHE CLAIMS THAT MUMPHRE KILLED HER HUSBAND!

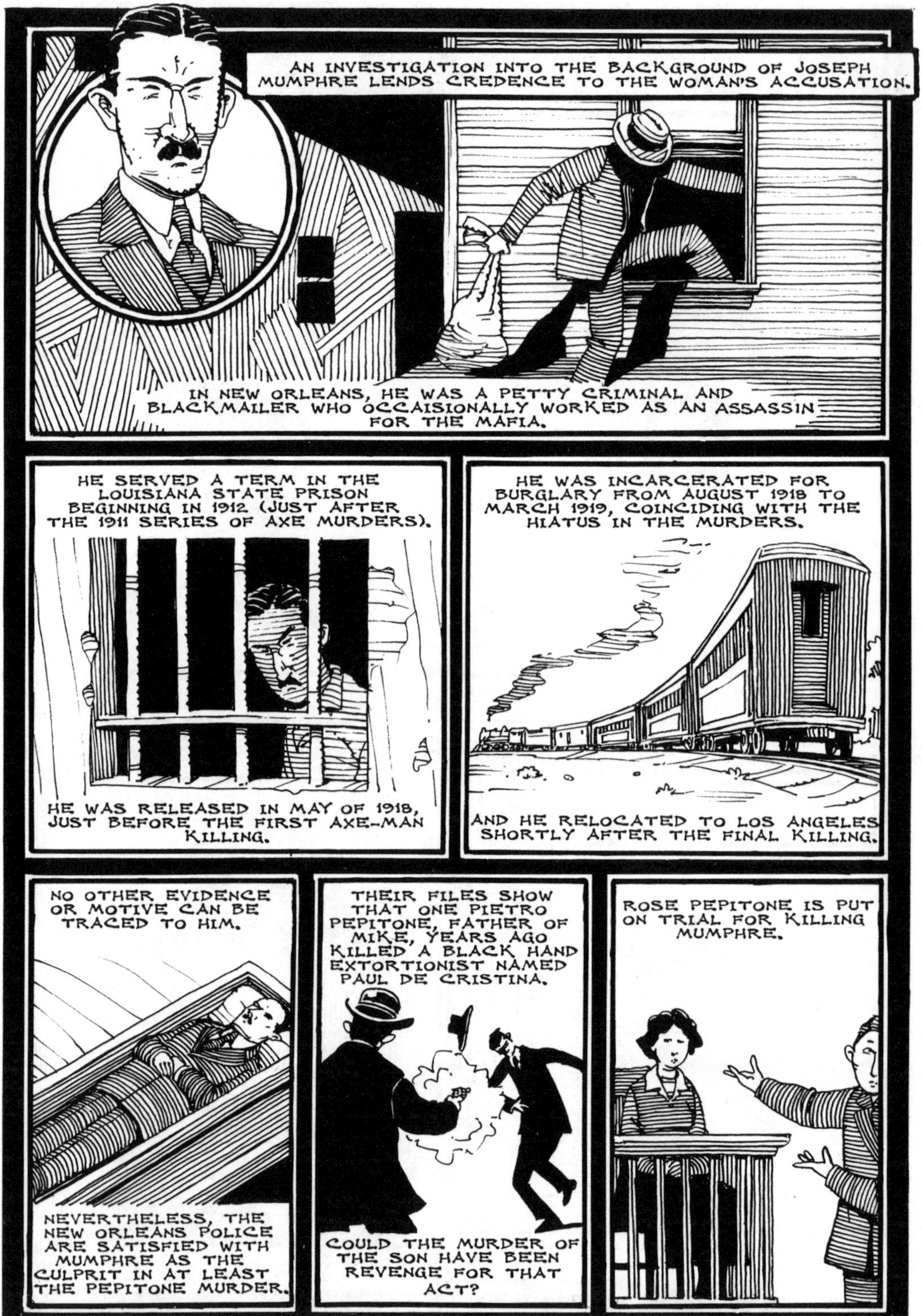
AN INVESTIGATION INTO THE BACKGROUND OF JOSEPH MUMPHRE LENDS CREDENCE TO THE WOMAN'S ACCUSATION.
IN NEW ORLEANS, HE WAS A PETTY CRIMINAL AND BLACKMAILER WHO OCCAISIONALLY WORKED AS AN ASSASSIN FOR THE MAFIA.
HE SERVED A TERM IN THE LOUISIANA STATE PRISON BEGINNING IN 1912 (JUST AFTER THE 1911 SERIES OF AXE MURDERS).
HE WAS RELEASED IN MAY OF 1918, JUST BEFORE THE FIRST AXE-MAN KILLING.
HE WAS INCARCERATED FOR BURGLARY FROM AUGUST 1918 TO MARCH 1919, COINCIDING WITH THE HIATUS IN THE MURDERS.
AND HE RELOCATED TO LOS ANGELES SHORTLY AFTER THE FINAL KILLING.
NO OTHER EVIDENCE OR MOTIVE CAN BE TRACED TO HIM.
NEVERTHELESS, THE NEW ORLEANS POLICE ARE SATISFIED WITH MUMPHRE AS THE CULPRIT IN AT LEAST THE PEPITONE MURDER.
THEIR FILES SHOW THAT ONE PIETRO PEPITONE, FATHER OF MIKE, YEARS AGO KILLED A BLACK HAND EXTORTIONIST NAMED PAUL DE CRISTINA.
COULD THE MURDER OF THE SON HAVE BEEN REVENGE FOR THAT ACT?
ROSE PEPITONE IS PUT ON TRIAL FOR KILLING MUMPHRE.

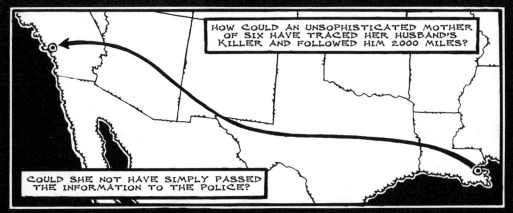

HOW COULD AN UNSOPHISTICATED MOTHER OF SIX HAVE TRACED HER HUSBAND'S KILLER AND FOLLOWED HIM 2000 MILES?

COULD SHE NOT HAVE SIMPLY PASSED THE INFORMATION TO THE POLICE?

SOME THEORIZE THAT SHE WAS CARRYING ON A LOVE AFFAIR WITH MUMPHRE.

THE TWO PLOTTED THE MURDER TOGETHER AND AFTERWARD, HE ABANDONED HER.

MRS. PEPITONE IS CONVICTED AND SENTENCED TO TEN YEARS IMPRISONMENT.

SHE IS RELEASED AFTER THREE YEARS...

AND PROMPTLY DISAPPEARS.

MONDAY, DECEMBER 6, 1920
ROSE CORTIMIGLIA RECANTS HER TESTIMONY AGAINST FRANK AND IORLANDO JORDANO.

SHE SAYS THAT ST. JOSEPH APPEARED TO HER IN A DREAM AND CONVINCED HER TO TELL THE TRUTH.

SHE ACCUSED THEM, SHE SAYS, OUT OF SPITE AND JEALOUSY, STEMMING FROM THE FAMILIES' LONG-STANDING FEUD.

FATHER AND SON ARE GIVEN FULL PARDONS AND SET FREE.

THE AXE-MAN MAY BE GONE . . .

BUT NOT SO THE SEVERAL PUZZLES SURROUNDING HIS IDENTITY.

AN EDITORIAL IN A LOCAL JOURNAL STATES THE PROBLEM SUCCINCTLY:

IS HE A MADMAN? A ROBBER? A VENDETTA AGENT? A SADIST? OR SOME MALIGN SUPERNATURAL SPIRIT?

IF A MADMAN, SO CUNNING AND DELIBERATE IN THE EXECUTION OF HIS CRIMES?

IF A ROBBER, WHY THE WANTON SHEDDING OF BLOOD . . .

WITH MONEY AND VALUABLES LEFT IN FULL VIEW?

IF A VENDETTA AGENT OF THE MAFIA, WHY INCLUDE AMONG HIS VICTIMS THOSE NOT UNDER THEIR SWAY?

(MOREOVER, THE MAFIA USUALLY FOREBEARS TO KILL WOMEN AND CHILDREN.)

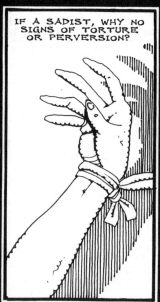
IF A SADIST, WHY NO SIGNS OF TORTURE OR PERVERSION?

FINALLY, IF HE IS A SPECTER OR SPIRIT, WHY IS THE FIGURE DESCRIBED BY WITNESSES AS BULKY AND SOLID?